Gamified Tabletop Exercises for Effective Disaster Recovery Testing

Preparing for Disasters with Dice

John Svazic

Apress®

Gamified Tabletop Exercises for Effective Disaster Recovery Testing:
Preparing for Disasters with Dice

John Svazic
Cambridge, ON, Canada

ISBN-13 (pbk): 979-8-8688-1251-4   ISBN-13 (electronic): 979-8-8688-1252-1
https://doi.org/10.1007/979-8-8688-1252-1

Managing Director, Apress Media LLC: Welmoed Spahr
Acquisitions Editor: Susan McDermott
Development Editor: Laura Berendson
Project Manager: Jessica Vakili

Cover designed by eStudioCalamar

Distributed to the book trade worldwide by Springer Science+Business Media New York, 1 New York Plaza, New York, NY 10004. Phone 1-800-SPRINGER, fax (201) 348-4505, e-mail orders-ny@springer-sbm.com, or visit www.springeronline.com. Apress Media, LLC is a Delaware LLC and the sole member (owner) is Springer Science + Business Media Finance Inc (SSBM Finance Inc). SSBM Finance Inc is a **Delaware** corporation.

For information on translations, please e-mail booktranslations@springernature.com; for reprint, paperback, or audio rights, please e-mail bookpermissions@springernature.com.

Apress titles may be purchased in bulk for academic, corporate, or promotional use. eBook versions and licenses are also available for most titles. For more information, reference our Print and eBook Bulk Sales web page at http://www.apress.com/bulk-sales.

If disposing of this product, please recycle the paper

To Tammy,

*I'll keep taking on the world as long as
I have your love and support. Thanks for everything;
it's been an amazing ride so far.*

To my children,

*Thank you for giving me the drive to move forward
with my dreams and giving me the courage to do so,
if only to try to make the world better for you.*

To the infosec community as a whole,

*I am nothing if not the product of my environments.
Thank you for your support and insights as I move
forward in trying to share the lessons I have learned
and give back to the wider community to help us all
achieve our goals.*

Table of Contents

About the Author

John Svazic is the CEO and principal consultant of EliteSec Information Security Consultants, a boutique information security consultancy near Toronto, Ontario, Canada. He has been writing and running gamified tabletops since 2017. He used to run an infosec podcast called *Purple Squad Security*, in which he had a few episodes running gamified tabletops with hosts from other infosec podcasts. He also had a talk at Tactical Edge 2020 and the True North 2018 where he led live tabletop exercises with volunteers.

John has been in the IT field for over 25 years, with the last 15 years focused on information security. He holds a number of certifications, including CISSP, CISM, OSCP, and others. His goal is to share knowledge and experience, as well as to get a bit more recognition for his efforts. He is not the first to try to gamify tabletops, but his approach is more user-friendly than others not in the infosec space.

About the Technical Reviewer

As the global director of threat research at Carbon Black, **Paul Miller** has over 20 years of experience in information security and a proven track record of analyzing, detecting, and responding to emerging cyber threats. He leads a team of experts who provide actionable intelligence and guidance to our customers and partners, leveraging our cloud-native endpoint and workload protection solutions.

Paul is also a director at Veilid Foundation Inc., a nonprofit organization that promotes online privacy and cyber education. He oversees the development and delivery of training programs, workshops, and events that teach and inspire the next generation of security professionals and enthusiasts. Paul is passionate about sharing his knowledge and skills in threat intelligence, penetration testing, endpoint security, and digital forensics. He also speaks fluent German and enjoys collaborating with diverse and talented teams across the globe.

About the Technical Reviewer

CHAPTER 1

Tabletops, Gamification, and Dice

A Quick Overview of Tabletop Exercises

Welcome to the world of gamified tabletops! Before we dive into the details of gamified tabletops, here's a quick recap of the purpose of tabletop exercises, how they work, and what are the elements of a traditional tabletop exercise. As gamified tabletops don't differ that much from traditional tabletop exercises, this refresher will give us a solid foundation for future discussions.

What Are They?

A tabletop exercise involves assembling key personnel responsible for emergency management roles and responsibilities to discuss simulated emergency scenarios in a nonthreatening setting. In other words, it's a means to get key employees together to discuss how they would handle an emergency that hits their company without having to deal with said situation. Consider it a type of fire drill to practice for the real thing.

© John Svazic 2025
J. Svazic, *Gamified Tabletop Exercises for Effective Disaster Recovery Testing*,
https://doi.org/10.1007/979-8-8688-1252-1_1

These exercises are often called "paper exercises," because they are more discussion focused rather than performing physical actions. The scenarios can vary from things like the office being flooded from a hurricane to a ransomware outbreak that encrypts key systems, rendering them useless.

Not all scenarios are technical in nature, and even technical scenarios will often have nontechnical elements to them, but we're getting a bit ahead of ourselves. The point is that a tabletop exercise is a chance to work out what needs to be done during an emergency while you have the time to think, discuss, and practice the steps required during an actual emergency.

Often during these exercises, someone is taking notes. This person, usually called *the scribe*, is going to take all manner of notes, to avoid breaking the flow of discussion with the other participants. The scribe is in general not one of the key personnel that is participating in the execution of the exercise.

A common tactic that I have used myself is to set up a conference call with all the participants and then record that call, only to transcribe things afterward. This allows you to focus on the exercise in the moment, and you don't risk losing any details because everything is recorded. This is also recommended if you can't find a reliable participant who wants to perform the scribe's role.

Another approach is to use something like Microsoft Copilot to transcribe the discussion. There are various plug-ins that can be used for various video conferencing software, so this approach may help with the review of the meeting later on without having to rewatch the entire recording.

Who Gets Invited?

Who are the "key personnel" invited to participate in a traditional tabletop? Well, these will be employees from finance, legal, IT, security, marketing, and possibly HR. They may be members of management or lower-level employees responsible for performing certain tasks. The purpose for each team's representation will depend on the disaster recovery/business continuity plan. For example, a marketing representative or an HR representative may seem odd for a tabletop exercise, but if the scenario for the exercise involves employee records, then their participation is going to be required. Likewise, if the scenario involves any form of external communication, then a representative from the marketing group should be involved.

Part of planning for a tabletop exercise is understanding who all should be involved. This is easy if an existing plan is already in place, but if not, then it's a bit more upfront work as you have to determine who to invite. We will go into this issue in more detail later in the book, but for now understand that it's much more than just technical folk or executives that should be involved. Striking a balance will make a noticeable difference in how well the exercise will be perceived in terms of value and success.

How Often Do They Run?

Once the team has been determined and a scheduled meeting has been set, the group will get together and go through the exercise. There will need to be an appointed leader for the exercise, someone to play the role of narrator who will step through the incident and essentially guide the conversations to ensure the team stays on track. This individual will start by reading aloud the starting point, such as all Internet and telecommunications systems at the main office going down for some yet unknown reason.

Next, this narrator may ask the group broadly on what should be done next or perhaps ask a specific person what the next steps should be. Normally, people will react to the situation and immediately go with a gut reaction, but a question that should be asked is "Do we have a plan for this?", and if yes, what is the procedure to identify and rectify the situation? If there is no plan yet, then a discussion is warranted. Keep in mind that the scribe will want to note this, so that at the end of the exercise, there will be a task to start working on a new disaster recovery plan based on the choices made during the exercise itself.

Can You "Lose" a Tabletop?

Since tabletop exercises are essentially practice exercises, some of you may wonder if there's a way to "fail" the exercise. There is always the possibility that you cannot find a solution for a given scenario, mainly due to lack of preparedness for the situation. This is common for ransomware scenarios where some type of crypt coin payment is required, but no one understands how to acquire the coins in the first place or whether or not it is against company policy. Then the question of regulation may come into play, such as a legal requirement to notify authorities of the breach. Does this mean the exercise was a failure? Quite the contrary, the fact that there is a gap in knowledge on how to handle this situation is a great outcome and should be considered a success! But why?

Isn't this a bad thing? Not at all, but the tabletop in this fabricated scenario has proven to be quite successful as it has uncovered some potential flaws in the processes in the handling of a ransomware scenario ahead of time and didn't cost the organization any time or effort in a time of crisis! This is one of the goals in a tabletop exercise, namely, to understand what to do when disasters hit the company and uncover any potential shortcomings beforehand so they can be addressed before such a situation arises.

What Is the Goal of a Tabletop Exercise?

Tabletop exercises are meant to be a type of practice session to go through the steps, actions, and activities that need to happen during an actual emergency. There are generally a few different goals, depending on the experience of the team participating in the exercise, both in terms of exposure to disasters as well as their experience in handling difficult situations such as a disaster scenario:

- To test an existing disaster recovery or business continuity plan, ensuring that it is accurate and sufficiently documented/detailed for employees to follow/refer to in the case of an actual emergency.

- To help create a new disaster recovery plan if one is not already written.

- If no disaster recovery/business continuity plan exists, then the steps taken during the tabletop exercise can be used to build up a new plan for the organization.

- To see how the key employees work together in case of an emergency, both in terms of communication as well as identification of key roles and responsibilities across the organization.

The last one is often the most important outcome of these exercises. Not knowing who is responsible for what can lead to a lot of wasted time and effort by the team, so understanding who is responsible for what ahead of time is critical.

What Happens at the End of a Tabletop Exercise?

Once a tabletop exercise is complete, a short review of the exercise is normally done. The team can have an open and honest discussion about the exercise and what they thought of it, how it could be improved in the future, and reiterate any takeaways and ensure that owners for each task are assigned. There may even be a follow-up tabletop exercise to continue if there is still more work to be done on the exercise, which is not uncommon for more complex scenarios.

A *postmortem* review is sometimes done after the tabletop with some members of the exercise to review what went well and what didn't, followed by suggestions on what should be done differently the next time around. Follow-up meetings should be done with team members to ensure tasks are completed as agreed upon.

How Long Do Tabletops Take to Run?

The average time to run a tabletop exercise is going to vary based on several factors, including

- The complexity of the scenario
- How prepared the team is for the scenario
- How much experience the team has in dealing with disasters
- The availability of the participants

It is not uncommon to split a tabletop exercise across multiple days just due to availability reasons. It is best to go if you can in one sitting to avoid missing out on details and spending the first part of subsequent meetings recapping what was done previously. It is not uncommon to spend two to four hours per tabletop meeting.

What's Wrong with Traditional Tabletops?

The traditional tabletop exercise clearly has a lot to offer, from helping define processes to practicing for actual disasters with individuals who will be handling the recovery. So what is wrong with them? To put it simply, they're boring.

If you've ever sat in on a technically focused tabletop exercise as a nontechnical person, or vice versa, you will know exactly what I mean. People will naturally tune in and listen to material that interests them but tune out other discussions as they either do not understand the terminology or feel it's not relevant to their position or job responsibilities. As such, context can be lost and the purpose of participating in the tabletop exercise may be questioned.

The other major problem with traditional tabletop exercises is that they are very linear and often follow what I like to call "the happy path." Basically, there is no adversary to any decision made. Take the example of a ransomware event. A "happy path" solution would be to simply ignore the ransom demand and restore from backup. Alternatively, the decision may be to let the insurance policy pay out the ransom. The first question should be, what if the backups are not available? What if they were deleted or corrupted because there's no history of testing those backups? Likewise, what if the insurance company denies the payment because they determine that the company failed to practice due care and due diligence in their cybersecurity controls, and thus no payment for the ransom will be provided?

Without these possible outcomes, lots of people will turn a blind eye and expect to have success because they know what needs to be done, and they cannot envision a scenario in which their solution would fail. Following "the happy path" during a tabletop exercise may lead to a false sense of preparedness and thus make things more difficult when an actual disaster strikes. This leads to the invention of gamified tabletops and introducing the concept of randomness to scenarios and decisions, but we'll get into more detail about that soon enough.

Why Dice?

When I speak with new clients about gamified tabletops, they often wonder why I insist on using dice to do the exercise itself. The answer is to introduce some randomness! It also brings a sense of familiarity to participants, since rolling dice is a common concept for most people.

I will cover the use of dice in more detail a bit later in the book, but for now suffice it to say that they serve a genuine purpose and can help both with the gamification of the tabletop (by introducing an element normally associated with board games) as well as a degree of control to avoid following "the happy path."

Many years ago, I worked for a company that offered bite-sized training programs wrapped in a gamified delivery system. Think of mini games played in a browser that would randomly pop up questions for you depending on some action within the game. It was an interesting concept that raised the desire for employees to want to participate in this daily training regime, and the results were measurable. As such, I decided that the standard tabletop exercise needed to have some element of gamification as well, but in a manner that is accessible to everyone. Thus, the introduction of dice to a tabletop exercise was born!

Gamification can help with engagement and excitement. It's also a nice, neutral way to have participants stay interested in what's going on with the exercise, as no one is sure of the outcome of a decision if a dice roll is required. Keeping up engagement while also exploring new possibilities is what makes gamification of tabletops unique and beneficial.

Other Types of Tabletop Exercises

I have spent a fair bit of time discussing traditional tabletop exercises where key personnel get together to work through a simulated crisis scenario, but there are alternative means to doing so. One of them is through a gamification process that we will explore in this book, but there are other examples that I would like to share.

Backdoors and Breaches is a card game from the good folks at Black Hills Information Security and Active Countermeasures. It is mainly aimed at providing scenarios and issues for incident response teams, mostly focused on the cybersecurity space. Highly technical in nature, it is another example of gamification for tabletop exercises.

Some of the larger consulting firms also offer more in-depth tabletop exercises, often running them in real time with a parallel set of communications channels, such as alternate email domains for communication and chat apps dedicated to the exercise itself. They will focus on real-time activities, meaning that the participants are not sitting in a meeting room but are instead going about their day when the "disaster" hits to see how they react. I was told a story about such an exercise where the CIO was on his way to his vacation destination with his family, only to receive the call while on the jet bridge leading to the plane. He had to leave his family to jump on the call. Now the timing wasn't accidental, the participants knew the timing of the exercise, but they purposefully waited to call him just before takeoff. Cold and calculated, but then not all disasters are conscientious of your schedule.

I have a friend who is currently working on a tabletop scenario generator based on ChatGPT that will drive outcomes based on user input to a given scenario, kind of like a choose your own adventure book, but using modern techniques. This is something that I will be keeping an eye on as well since it is a rather unique and novel approach.

Tabletop exercises can take many forms, and there is no single approach that works for everyone or every scenario. We will go through the steps of using gamification for tabletops of all types, but the examples will lean more toward cybersecurity-based threats or other technology-based scenarios. Rest assured, if you have the domain knowledge for other types of threats, these same techniques can be applied to those scenarios as well.

CHAPTER 2

Roles, Rules, and Goals

What Are the Roles in a Gamified Tabletop?

While key personnel are invited to participate in a tabletop exercise due to their role within the organization, they will also fall into a particular role during the tabletop exercise itself. By defining specific roles in the exercise, participants can better understand what's expected of them and their peers. Let's dive into the different types of roles.

The Scribe

In the last chapter, we discussed the idea of a scribe role that will take notes during the tabletop exercise and the potential to replace this role and responsibility with the record function of modern video conferencing platforms such as Zoom and Microsoft Teams. This will simplify things, but it is still important to have someone review the recordings and summarize the experience.

If hiring an external consulting firm, this duty falls upon their staff. If not, then someone should be handed the responsibility of reviewing and summarizing the tabletop exercise. This should be provided to all

© John Svazic 2025
J. Svazic, *Gamified Tabletop Exercises for Effective Disaster Recovery Testing*,
https://doi.org/10.1007/979-8-8688-1252-1_2

participants and discussed in a separate meeting to ensure everyone is on the same page and define what new tasks and deliverables should be created and assigned based on this review.

The focus of the scribe is to make note of not just the decisions being made during the exercise but also how well the discussions are going between the participants. Is there someone who is dominating the discussion? Someone whose input was ignored? Someone who was not paying attention? These points are not to call out any individual, but to ensure that all participants are fully engaged and respectful of one another. A dominant personality may lead a tabletop exercise when things are calm, but what happens during an actual disaster and that individual is not available? Ensuring there is adequate coverage and separation of duties is paramount to ensuring a successful recovery during a disaster. Overreliance on one person is never a good plan. Likewise, having disconnected or otherwise uninterested participants may indicate that they feel undervalued or otherwise unheard from, which may also be disastrous during an incident if they withhold information or offer key advice because they feel isolated.

Ensuring that all participants are heard and are participating in their own respective roles during a tabletop exercise is very important. Having these interactions noted can help strengthen the rapport and communications between the participants prior to an actual event.

The Participant

The participant role is for anyone who is actively participating in the tabletop exercise itself. Their goal is to work through the challenges facing the group, as well as to collaborate and support other participants. While they cannot determine the outcome of their decisions, their job is to focus on what decisions need to be made and ask questions to determine next steps.

What a participant cannot do is question whether a scenario or outcome from a decision makes sense or is viable. They are there to react to situations, not try to upsend the exercise. I have had this happen in tabletops myself in the past. I once had a person claim that they were going to resign rather than deal with a situation, wherein they were informed that their resignation was not approved and their participation was required, but it gave me an idea for future scenarios.

Participants are the main players in the exercise itself. It is important that no other roles interfere with the participants and let them make their own decisions, either on their own or by following a preexisting plan. Criticism of decisions, etc., should not be done during the exercise, but constructive feedback can be shared during the postmortem.

The Conductor

The conductor role can go by many different names, such as the leader, storyteller, narrator, "dungeon master" or DM for those familiar with dungeons and dragon's tabletop games, and so forth. This is the individual who is conducting the tabletop exercise itself. Their job is to provide the scenario and the consequences for decisions made by the participants to a given obstacle. They are neutral in the grand scheme of things, simply relaying events as they unfold during the exercise and answering questions to the best of their ability, without delving into details not yet exposed.

This is probably the most crucial role for the entire exercise and is normally handled by someone who is familiar with how the team would react to a given disaster to help guide the participants accordingly. There is no hard requirement that this be someone from outside the organization. Their only requirement is that they are not involved in the tabletop exercise at all in terms of being a participant. They must remain neutral in both execution and decision-making by the participants, but they can "move along" the discussion if the participants are at an impasse and are not progressing through the exercise.

Note that this is the most important role in the tabletop exercise. Not only will this individual drive the exercise but also ensure that the participants follow the rules of the exercise and other rules set forth at the start of the tabletop exercise itself.

The Observer

The observer role is applied to individuals who are joining the tabletop exercise but will not participate in any discussions or decisions at any point. There are instances when a senior executive may want to observe how the team will handle an incident, and they want to observe but not directly participate. While not something I would normally encourage, this is a valid role for such an individual.

The reason I don't recommend having an observer in a tabletop exercise is because their presence may cause an interruption to the natural flow of the other participants, due to a sense of anxiety from "doing the wrong thing," especially if the observer is in their management chain. Having individuals reacting differently based on the presence of an observer is a negative point in the decision to invite such personnel to the tabletop exercise.

As a compromise, sharing the recording of the exercise with observers who wish to review how the exercise was handled may be a better option. This way, they can react as they want without the risk of influencing any of the participants. Feedback can be provided as necessary without the fear of influencing how the exercise itself was performed.

Observers can be a useful role to have as an independent observer of the interaction between groups to look for potential breakdowns in communication or teamwork. This is something that larger firms may have within the tabletop exercise itself, especially for more complex engagements that we discussed in the last chapter.

If you have an observer who is in a leadership role within the company, then it's best to ensure this person does not have any ties to the reporting structure of the participants if possible; otherwise, their presence will be more of a distraction instead. Offer the recordings to these individuals instead, so they are not distracting the participants but can still observe the exercise after the fact.

Rules to Keep Everyone in Sync

Since tabletop exercises are interactive and open communication is encouraged, it is important to set some ground rules for all participants to abide by for a few reasons. First, it helps to ensure that the exercise goes smoothly. Next, they can help to ensure that the exercise can be considered "successful" by avoiding getting dragged down into obscure discussions that may detail the exercise itself.

As for the rules themselves, there are only a few. More rules may be added as deemed appropriate, but it would be best to keep the list small to avoid overwhelming the participants. That and in a professional situation with participants from a given profession, there shouldn't be a need to go overboard.

The Rules

Rules for a tabletop exercise are small and simple. Most of these should be self-explanatory or expected by default, but it never hurts to list them out explicitly.

1. Be respectful of all participants and their views.

2. Treat the exercise as a real event and make decisions accordingly.

3. Suspend your disbelief; this is an exercise that uses a mock disaster.

In general, it is advisable to bring attention to these rules at the start of the exercise, to ensure that everyone is on the same page. I have had some unique experiences in the past during tabletop exercises where these rules needed to be repeated. The last rule is usually the biggest sticking point.

In a later chapter, we will go over scenario selection and what is all involved, but I do want to raise this as a potential sticking point early on, so that you can be prepared for it. Nearly every tabletop I have ever hosted has had a comment, question, or criticism over an aspect of the tabletop that was considered "impossible" or "not realistic" for whatever reason. Not by everyone, but generally by one person who is often skeptical of the entire exercise. Can you go overboard with the scenario selection? Of course, but there are ways to get around that.

My advice when it comes to communicating these rules with the participants is that these are set in stone, and that any concerns can be raised afterward. Again, the point of a tabletop exercise, gamified or not, is to try to work through a disaster scenario to the best of the team's capabilities, not to question whether such an event is even possible. If it's not possible, then explain why it's not possible. How sure are you that everything will work out exactly as you expect? This is the reason for rule 3.

One great example of this is when the group is working through a ransomware scenario. In general, someone will say that they will just restore from backup, so what's the problem? Well, what if the backup restoration failed? "That can't happen!" Are you sure? Have you tested it? How often? What assurances do you have that they are impossible to fail? Testing can only go so far, and while the likelihood of a restoration failing may be low based on past testing, it is not zero. That's the point, and this is why we include a rule to suspend disbelief of an event during a tabletop exercise, because such discussions will only distract from the task at hand and potentially deride the entire exercise, benefitting no one. Not only that, when something like a backup restoration does fail, the team won't know what else to do because the "impossible" scenario has become reality.

The conductor should be focused on ensuring that these rules are being adhered to during the tabletop exercise, but each participant should feel empowered to keep their peers in check as well.

Goals: What Is Considered Done?

When is a tabletop exercise finished? When the timer runs out or something else? That's a great question, and like all good questions, the answer is a simple one – it depends. The overall purpose of a tabletop exercise is to walk through a given disaster scenario in a controlled environment to determine how to overcome the issue. Does it end when the disaster is contained or overcome? Maybe, but oftentimes there is additional work afterward to help. Remember, overcoming an issue to get back to a working state may mean something very different than being back to full capacity and capability for the organization.

This is a great starting point and one that should be decided on and communicated at the start of the exercise, i.e., is the goal to overcome the issue such that the organization can get back to a functioning state, or do you want to get back to 100% capacity and capability? The former is easier to accomplish, but the latter is going to be more complete. My recommendation would be to focus on the latter unless you already have post-event plans in terms of cleanup that have been documented and tested separately. While it may take longer, it will pay off in the long run and can be an infrequent addition to the tabletop if it is deemed excessive.

The other assumption to be aware of, especially with gamified tabletop exercises, is the belief/expectation that the tabletop exercise will "end" on a clean or successful note. There is the probability, however small, that the exercise itself will result in a failure. What's a failure? Not being able to recover in a timely manner negatively impacts the ability for the organization to function properly in a reasonable timeline. This is going to vary depending on the organization of course. An organization with razor-thin margins but operating in a high-frequency environment may not be able to afford any significant downtime versus a software vendor that can handle an outage of the main systems for a few hours. Context matters, but it will be beneficial for everyone to define this early.

Failure Can Be Inevitable

Failure to handle a scenario is not always a bad thing, nor should it be viewed as a failure of the exercise or the participants. Quite the contrary, the exercise was successful in finding deficiencies in the plans, processes, or knowledge of the organization or participants that can now be actioned upon! In fact, this is a valid outcome as it did help understand the potential pitfalls for a given disaster in a controlled environment, rather than when a disaster strikes, and you are completely unprepared.

Take caution, however, if the reason for the failure was not related to a gap in knowledge, experience, or capabilities but rather through arguments, apathy, or general miscommunication. "The road to hell is paved with good intentions" is a phrase that seems fitting here. For example, if you are working through a scenario where your critical business systems are ransomed, and you cannot move forward without recovering these systems from backup or some other means, but you have a CEO or CFO who refuses to pay the ransom on principle alone, then you may hit a stalemate. If the conductor finds this type of situation occurs during a tabletop exercise, it may be best to pause the exercise and offer to discuss this point further with some key decision-makers to justify the stance or to at least evaluate further what this means to the organization.

This isn't as far-fetched as you may believe. There is a reason that the rule about suspending your disbelief is one of our few rules, because this will often be the excuse used to justify such a stance. "It just won't happen!" is usually the answer. Sure, it won't happen – until it does. And when it does, what will you do? How will you proceed? Do you want to be prepared for an eventuality that may never occur or just hope that it never happens and then try to work through it without preparation when it eventually does occur?

Emotions tend to run high during these discussions, so again pausing or ending the exercise and then regrouping the following day to discuss is recommended, to let people reset and come to the follow-up discussions with clear and open minds, on both sides of the argument.

In general, failure is not a bad thing, but it doesn't mean it should be accepted as inevitable. Working through the decisions to find out the reason for the failure is going to be important, as you will be able to determine what should be changed to avoid this outcome. There is almost always a reason for a negative outcome to occur, but the question is how can you prevent it from happening should a similar issue come to fruition?

Success may be the complete resolution of the issue at hand. This may be restoration of key systems, return to a functioning state, expulsion of an adversary from an internal system, etc. If the majority of participants agree that the issue at the heart of the tabletop exercise has been overcome, then the exercise can be declared to be at an end.

A follow-up meeting should be held to review the report of how the exercise itself went and what could be done better. Even if the exercise was considered successful, it wouldn't hurt to ask the question "what could be done better?" There is almost always something that could be improved upon. Any postmortem discussions should both praise the success of the participants and ask this question in order to help improve things. If no improvements could be found, then perhaps a different scenario should be used for future exercises. This is common if an organization focuses on the same disaster for each exercise. This can lead to a false sense of security because preparedness for one situation may lead to the belief that the organization can handle *any* situation, but unfortunately this isn't always accurate. For example, being prepared to handle the breach resulting in the loss of customer data may not be enough to prepare you for the flooding of an office or data center that impacts your employees.

When to Wrap Things Up

There are situations that may arise that will require a premature end of the tabletop exercise itself. These may be unavoidable, but understanding what happens next is also important. Note that wrapping up a tabletop session does not mean completion of the entire exercise, but it could be used to break it up into multiple sessions if more steps are required. Do not end an exercise unless your main goals have been achieved. This is why it is so important to define these goals ahead of time.

Time Constraints

If the allocated time for the discussion is coming to an end, then make note of where the state of the situation is in, and try to schedule a follow-up meeting as soon as possible to complete the exercise. It may be tempting to say that things are "good enough" and no follow-up is necessary, but this should be agreed upon by all participants to ensure nothing was missed, or if there's a lingering question or sense of uncertainty from someone due to an item not being addressed.

Always go back and reevaluate the original time allocated and determine why it wasn't sufficient. Was there more discussion than expected? Were people focused on figuring out what to do in a given situation? Did you underestimate the time required? All of these are valid reasons to end early, but the key is to agree to a continuation session soon to continue the exercise.

Lack of Preparation/Knowledge/Experience

A situation may arise where none of the participants knows what to do next. A key vendor has gone down, but no one knows how to contact them. A bitcoin payment is required, but no one knows how to buy any. This is not necessarily a fault of the participants, but rather a gap in knowledge they did not know they had! Situations such as these are examples of valid reasons to pause the current tabletop exercise session and pick up again in the future when such issues are understood and can be overcome. Establish a timeframe for resolution and make sure a follow-up session is scheduled before adjourning the session, to ensure that the exercise can reach some type of a natural resolution.

It is important to understand, especially for participants who may never have done a tabletop exercise before or for a company that doesn't have a disaster recovery plan in place, that this is much more common than not. This does not mean that the participants are incapable in any way; rather, it just highlights that there are gaps in existing knowledge and plans that may need some further follow-up.

Emotional Distress

Tabletop exercises can get very intense and very involved, depending on the disaster being evaluated and how committed the participants are to the exercise. Some folks may take things personally, to the point of experiencing some form of emotional distress such as panic attacks. The conductor should be on alert for such developments and offer a recess or short break as necessary to calm things down. If the participants are arguing with each other and there is a general sense of confrontation between them, then another break may be warranted.

Having a passionate view of the scenario and how to best approach the situation is admirable, but if folks are getting carried away with it, then a pause is in order. Postponing the remainder of the exercise may be in everyone's best interest if things cannot be brought back under control.

Main Actions Completed

A tabletop exercise may be determined to be completed when the main recovery actions were completed, such as restoration of lost data, the reopening of a location, etc. There may be smaller tasks that need to be completed, but they are not critical or complex enough to warrant continuation of the exercise, or they are so routine that even if something goes awry, the participants already know how to handle the situation. In these cases, it may be best to wrap up the exercise and simply make note of the remaining tasks that are to be considered routine and can be dealt with accordingly.

CHAPTER 3

Gamified Tabletops: An Overview

We've looked at the process by which a standard tabletop exercise is executed, from the different roles of the participants to how and when to wrap up an exercise. What we haven't yet touched on is the idea of a *gamified* tabletop exercise. What is gamification? Why should a tabletop be gamified? What's the benefit? What issues may you run into with gamification? Does this make the tabletop exercises more complex and difficult for the participants?

This chapter is where we will explore what the concept behind gamification is, why it works, and how to apply it to nearly any type of tabletop exercise. We will explore the concepts and techniques and even include some tips for introducing gamification mechanics to participants.

How Are They Different?

Gamified tabletops are a method to introduce an element of randomness and fun into what can often be seen as a boring and dull exercise. The risk is that participants in a normal tabletop may lose interest in the activity if they are not actively participating or have no interest in actions being done by another participant that does not involve them. I have personally

© John Svazic 2025
J. Svazic, *Gamified Tabletop Exercises for Effective Disaster Recovery Testing*,
https://doi.org/10.1007/979-8-8688-1252-1_3

witnessed this on more than a few occasions, and it was something that always bothered me. As such, the idea of adding a *gamified* element to tabletop exercises was born.

What Is Gamification?

To quote Karl Kapp, a leader in gamified learning and gamification principles:

> *Gamification is using game-based mechanics, aesthetics and game thinking to engage people, motivate action, promote learning, and solve problems.*

When it comes to gamified tabletops, the game-based mechanic we will be introducing is the concept of rolling dice for certain decisions to see what the outcome will be for that decision. This is a simple concept that helps to introduce randomness to the exercise itself, cannot be easily predicted by participants, and helps maintain focus and interest from other participants as they await the results.

The use of dice is not just reminiscent of traditional tabletop games but brings a sense of randomness and uncertainty to the tabletop exercise. This will raise a sense of intrigue in the participants as they are curious about what happens after each roll of the die.

Why Use Gamification?

Now that we understand that we're going to add some dice to our tabletop exercises, the next logical question is why do it in the first place? As mentioned previously, the goal for gamification is multifaceted; we want to avoid "the happy path" during the exercise where everything just works out and no real challenges are faced, and we want to engage all the participants during the exercise, even if they are not currently involved in a given action or procedure.

Avoiding "the happy path" is the main factor here. It can be very tempting to simply believe that a particular solution will just work and therefore there is no reason to question its applicability. For example, contacting someone is just going to work because you have their personal mobile phone number, so why would you need anyone else's number? Why would you not be able to contact them? Surely, they will be always available when something happens, right? Sadly, things rarely go smoothly or as expected. A mobile phone may not be charged, be turned off, be out of a service area, or simply not heard when ringing. The individual may be on vacation or unable to assist even if they are able to communicate because they need to physically be available to participate. As such, these types of issues need to be considered and alternatives discussed before an actual situation arises. This is the heart of a tabletop exercise – to prepare for disasters in a controlled environment where such questions can be asked.

Most people are optimists and do not want to always believe in worst-case scenarios. Pessimists may be more inclined to think of the worst possible outcome in any given situation or decision, but such negativity is not welcomed and is often overlooked and dismissed with the phrase "Well, that would never happen!" until it does happen. Saying "I told you so" also does not help with the situation in the heat of the moment. So, what is the balance between too much optimism and too much pessimism? Trying to have a healthy mix between the two.

Humans are bad at generating randomness. We like to think that we're better than we are, but the truth is that we really suck at it. As such, we should externalize the need to randomize the good and bad outcomes as much as possible. This is where the idea of dice comes into play. Why not use the roll of a die to determine the outcome of a decision, be it good or bad? It is a small change, but it does help introduce this element of randomness without falling prey to being overly optimistic or pessimistic.

In addition to introducing a random element into the outcomes for a given decision, we now have a new mechanic that offers other participants interest in what will happen when a die is rolled by someone. Whereas in a traditional tabletop exercise, a participant may decide, for the most part other participants not directly involved in either the decision-making or the outcome of said decision may "tune out" of the process as there is no interest for them to participate. As such, key events may be missed, and the effectiveness of the exercise may diminish.

There is a German word, Schadenfreude, which essentially translates to taking joy over some harm or misfortune suffered by another. When the potential outcome of a decision may be negative, interest in the outcome of a die roll instantly draws the attention of other participants. I have personally had experiences where this interest has generated a different outcome based on feedback by other participants who vocalized what they considered to be either a good or bad outcome. But we will cover this in more detail later on when we go deeper into the mechanics of dice rolling to determine outcomes. The point is that other participants become invested in the outcome of a dice roll for someone else, causing them to be more attentive and aware of the exercise. And that really is the point, is it not? As such, this simple gamification mechanic is a great way to improve on a traditional tabletop exercise.

How Complicated Are They?

Gamified versions of traditional tabletop exercises are not very complicated from the perspective of the participants. If anything, they become more fun and enjoyable due to the randomness that can occur during the exercise! The only gamification mechanic being introduced is the rolling of a die.

However, it would be disingenuous to claim that there is no additional complexity when it comes to gamified tabletops, at least when it comes to the preparation of the exercise itself. Truth be told, there is a lot more preparation involved for the exercise itself. Normally, this is something that the conductor is responsible for. The tabletop exercise itself should be "scripted" ahead of time by outlining a few key items:

- What is the primary disaster facing the group?

- What secondary issues, such as smaller disasters, or other events that may hit during the exercise?

- What is considered the success criteria for the resolution of the disaster?

- How realistic is the disaster itself to the business?

- How are all participants and their respective groups/ departments involved in the resolution process?

When it comes to even a traditional tabletop, these are key factors to keep in mind when designing the tabletop exercise itself. You want to ensure that the disaster is something that could be genuinely faced by the business and that the groups involved in the tabletop exercise will be involved in the resolution. You also want to understand when the exercise is determined to be done/successfully resolved, so knowing this goal in the beginning is also important.

So how exactly does gamification increase the complexity in this design? Some tabletop designers will consider the types of decisions that participants may make ahead of time and use their own experience to determine whether or not those decisions are successful or not, either because of fact or false assumptions made during the exercise. However, for gamified tabletops, this decision takes a different turn.

Not every decision made by a participant will be successful or the right decision at the time. As such, anticipating decisions to be made by the participants is an important step/skill when building our exercises. Not only that, understanding the possible outcomes (both good and bad) is required. Personally, I like to think of at least three possible outcomes for a given decision: success, neutral, and failure. We will go into more detail about this in future chapters, but the point is that there may be multiple paths for decisions made by the participants. This is where the complexity comes into play, as it often falls back to the experience of the tabletop author to determine the different outcomes.

In short, the complexity of a gamified tabletop isn't in the execution of the exercise itself when compared to traditional tabletop exercises, but rather in the preparation and building of the gamified tabletop itself. We will provide a lot more guidance for this process in future chapters, but for now suffice it to say that the complexity is front-loaded in the process, not in the execution or post-exercise phases.

Outline of a Gamified Tabletop Exercise

As mentioned earlier, the game mechanic being introduced to gamified tabletops is the use of dice. Specifically, two dice will be used: a standard six-sided die (to be abbreviated as 1D6 for the remainder of the book) and a twenty-sided die (abbreviated as 1D20) normally used for tabletop games like *Dungeons & Dragons*. The purpose for each die will be covered shortly as they each serve a specific purpose but suffice it to say that both will be used in a gamified tabletop exercise.

Since the approach for a gamified tabletop is different from traditional tabletop exercises, I wanted to provide a brief outline of the way I like to run such exercises with a new group. Specifically, how I like to introduce the idea of the dice rolling to the participants, including some simple scenarios that can be used to introduce the concept.

Introduction

The first thing I like to do is have an introductory discussion to go over the purpose of the exercise, what we hope to accomplish, and the rules of the exercise itself. In Chapter 2, we discussed the goals and rules for tabletop exercises, so this is a great time to verbalize them to the participants and ensure that they are understood and agreed upon by everyone.

Kick-Off

Once the introduction is done, then the conductor should select one of the participants to get started. This can be someone who volunteers or is selected at random, it's up to the conductor to decide. I suggest starting with a simple scenario to showcase the dice rolling mechanic. Some ideas that can be used here:

- Ask for the participant's favorite sports team and say that they played a game recently, then ask them to roll a 1D6. If the roll is between 1–3, then the team lost. If the roll is between 4–6, then the team won!

- Ask the participant if they drink coffee or tea in the morning and how they take it. Then ask them to roll a 1D6. Again, a roll between 1–3 will result in the order being made incorrectly (missing/adding an ingredient), while a roll between 4–6 results in a perfect order that ends up being free due to some in-store promotion.

- Ask the participant how long their commute is to the office each morning, if they don't work from home. They will often give the time with and without traffic. Again, using a 1D6, have them roll. If the roll is between

1–3, then they hit traffic, and it takes a few minutes longer. Maybe due to an accident that causes a backup. If the roll is between 4–6, then there is lighter than usual traffic and they make some great time, arriving early enough that they can stop by the local coffee shop to get some breakfast treat before heading into the office.

These are just some examples of how you can introduce the dice rolling mechanic as part of the tabletop exercise. The "bad" outcome should be minor, but enough of an unwanted outcome that everyone realizes this is not something to be desired. Likewise, the "good" outcome should be desirable but not extravagant.

Starting the Exercise

With the introduction done and the example of the dice rolling established, it's time to begin. The conductor should continue with the establishment of the day, followed by an initial event that is of concern, but may not give away the exact issue at hand right away. For example:

You make your way to your desk and start to settle in for the day. <Participant name>, when you check your desk phone you notice quite a few voicemail messages waiting for you. As you start listening to the messages, there are a few employees (say 5 or more) who have called in claiming that they have no Internet access and cannot connect outside of the office. What do you want to do?

This introduction to the situation will vary depending on what the actual event is that you want to simulate. It's also possible to start with a smaller, simpler event to get the ball rolling before introducing a larger event that is what really needs to be overcome. In later chapters, we will go into more detail, but the main point is to start with a bit of background and some initial indications that something is wrong, and then selecting a participant who may be one of the first responders to whatever the issue may be causing.

You may want to select the same person who did the introduction to the dice rolling mechanic or someone else. This is up to the conductor to choose as it is not vital at this point of the exercise.

Working Through the Exercise

Throughout the rest of the exercise, the participants will continue to work through the different issues that come up, and out of those decisions, approximately 40–60% will have dice rolls associated with them.

This is an important point – **not every choice requires a dice roll**. Why not? Gamification and game mechanics should be viewed as a type of seasoning applied to the traditional tabletop exercise, so think of the dice rolls as salt. You don't want to oversalt your food when you're cooking, or you ruin the dish. The same applies to using game mechanics when gamifying a tabletop exercise. Having to roll a die for every decision will make participants question what the point of making any decision is, if every decision could be left to chance. There will be certain decisions that are just fixed in their outcome and as such do not require the roll of a die. In later chapters, we will explore this issue and offer some heuristics to help with determining which decisions should have a dice roll associated with them.

One example we can use here is if there is a gap in determining what to do next, such as not having an action or state defined in a playbook or part of the disaster recovery (DR) plan. These pauses are often great candidates for introducing a dice roll, but again use them sparingly.

Too much gamification and the mechanic will feel forced on the participants. Not enough and you risk it being viewed by the participants as a gimmick and not really offering anything of value. There is a happy medium, but it takes some experience and ideas on when it can be most effective. These are things that we will cover in detail shortly.

Finishing Up

Wrapping up the exercise itself is no different in a gamified tabletop versus a traditional tabletop exercise. There's no need for any special mechanics when wrapping up the exercise itself. Simply reiterating what the disaster event was, how it was resolved (successfully or not), and thanking participants for going through the exercise is enough.

I have had groups ask if it is possible that no solution can be achieved at all due to constantly rolling poor numbers and thus resulting in the worst-case scenario each time a die is rolled. Probability theory, specifically the law of large numbers, states that this is highly unlikely, but not impossible. In later chapters, we will address what to do if the exercise does start to sway in this type of direction, but suffice it to say that while not impossible, it is highly improbable that the worst-case scenario for every decision occurs.

Following up with a postmortem discussion on how the exercise went, lessons learned, general feedback, etc., should be done afterward as well. This feedback should be included in a final report summarizing the exercise. If the session needs to be broken up into multiple meetings, so be it. Chapter 2 covered some possible reasons for this, so it won't hurt to remind participants that they may not conclude in a single session. In a real-time scenario, it may take much longer to overcome a disaster, so simulating the recovery from a disaster may also take longer than a few hours, and that is perfectly normal.

Summary

Gamified tabletop exercises can be incredibly useful to improve engagement with participants as well to avoid following "the happy path" when executing the exercise. By adding an element of randomness, and the idea of *schadenfreude*, most participants will want to see what happens to their compatriots when a dice roll is made. Such interest keeps people involved and in tune with the exercise itself.

Gamification introduces randomness to the exercise and ensures that not everything will go as smoothly as expected, much as it does in a real-life situation. Providing a gentle introduction to the dice rolling mechanic can help ease nerves and promote an understanding of how to proceed with the rest of the exercise. The conductor should be the team member leading these activities, including prompting participants to roll the die based on a decision that they have made.

Not every decision requires a dice roll, as excessive dice rolling will distract from the main purpose of the exercise and breed questions and possible resentment toward the mechanic itself as being too much of a gimmick and not actually useful. Likewise, too few rolls may also be seen as introducing more of a gimmick to the exercise rather than something useful. Further chapters will explore this topic in greater detail.

Wrapping up the exercise itself should be done when the main goal has been achieved. While it is possible to end an exercise without properly resolving the issue at hand, this is a very rare occurrence and may warrant further discussions and review of the disaster faced and the decisions made to see if additional resources or training is needed before attempting again.

CHAPTER 4

Building the Exercise

With the foundation set for what a tabletop is, what the roles are, and some tips on running the exercise, it's time to start building out the content of the exercise itself. In this chapter, we're going to dive into the heart of tabletop exercise design, building out the scenario and what we expect to occur during the exercise, and share how to incorporate some branching mechanics, i.e., multiple choices, which will come in handy later. Finally, we will go over some suggestions and recommendations to make a compelling tabletop exercise that not only brings value to the participants, but that they will enjoy as well.

Scenario Selection

The very first place to start any sort of tabletop exercise design is figuring out what your scenario is going to be. In other words, what's the problem that the participants are going to overcome? This can be something generic or specific to the organization at hand. The most important thing is that it is realistic. Crafting a scenario about a group of terrorists taking over your office building may be great for a movie script, but not necessarily realistic in most situations.

© John Svazic 2025
J. Svazic, *Gamified Tabletop Exercises for Effective Disaster Recovery Testing*,
https://doi.org/10.1007/979-8-8688-1252-1_4

To get you started, here are some generic scenarios that are popular choices if you're just starting out:

- Ransomware outbreak

- Lost/stolen laptop containing sensitive information that was not encrypted

- Blizzard/tornado/earthquake/flood of main office

- Extended interruption at primary data center beyond your control

- Misconfigured cloud storage exposing customer data discovered by a researcher who published the report publicly

- Social gaffe by a senior company executive

- Breach by a trusted vendor/third party closely associated with your business

This is just a short list of examples. One quick observation is that not all scenarios are technical in nature, i.e., natural disasters can be legitimate scenarios for a tabletop exercise.

Outside of this list, there are a few other resources that you may want to consider. For example, when I'm working with clients, I will often start by asking them what keeps them up at night, i.e., what is something that's on the back of their minds that concerns them, but isn't a large enough problem to act on right now? Often, they have an answer for this question. Based on that answer, we build out a scenario for them. This is a fantastic method for coming up with a scenario for a tabletop exercise as it is often more relatable and thus resonates better with the participants.

If you are looking for something else, then news headlines are another great source for inspiration for scenario selection. Major outages that are newsworthy are great catalysts to ask the questions "What about us? How would we be impacted? What would we do in this situation?" Again, using the experience of others is not something to be overlooked for yourself!

A great online resource is the @badthingsdaily account on x.com (formerly known as Twitter). The author provides a wonderful list of possible tabletop scenarios, based on events from other organizations and the author's own experiences. It's a great source for tabletop scenarios, but some of them can be a bit extreme for most businesses. Some generic examples from this account are

- Classified documents are being distributed publicly from your servers.

- Leadership has asked your team to treat half the company as a potential insider threat.

- In the process of switching banks to avoid a bank run, finance realizes a former employee has the signature authority for bank transfers.

- A customer has escalated their suspicion that an employee at your company has accessed their data with an intent to profit from it.

- The administrator account to your organization's cloud email is no longer accessible. The recovery email belongs to a former employee on a custom domain running on a personal email server.

Some of these scenarios may be a bit out of reality but are often a great discussion point when determining where to begin.

Personally, I like to use the scenario of something realistic that could impact your business, either functionally, financially, or reputationally. Why? Because 99% of the time these are the major categories that may occur, and participants may feel more comfortable if they agree that they are possible issues they may face.

Asking employees (maybe not the direct pool of participants) for ideas is another great avenue to finding issues. Along the lines of "what keeps you up at night," asking employees from different departments will give you a new perspective as opposed to just sticking with a technical group. What could hurt the Sales or Marketing departments? What about HR? Support? The IT, Development, and Security teams will give clear technical concerns, but these other groups often have other concerns that many individuals may not ever think about. These are also some of the most interesting discussions, as these are not things that these teams often worry about. Raising awareness even before a tabletop exercise begins is always a bonus in my opinion.

So, to summarize, when determining a scenario for a tabletop exercise, try to remember these simple rules:

1. Ensure the scenario is realistic for the organization.

2. Try to pick a broad scenario that has multiple steps for resolution.

    a. If it's too simple, the exercise may be viewed as a waste of time, i.e., avoid the happy path scenarios because they're too simple.

3. Use other sources for scenario ideas, but the best scenarios are ones that the participants can relate to and believe are plausible.

Sample Scenario

Before we get too far ahead of ourselves, let's choose a sample scenario to work with. For the rest of this chapter, we will use the following scenario from the @badthingsdaily account:

An employee is repeatedly receiving MFA push notifications.

With a scenario in mind, the next step is building the actual tabletop exercise itself. This is where things get interesting.

Determine the Root Cause

Depending on the scenario you come up with, the starting point may be a symptom of a larger problem. This is very common with more technical scenarios, and it can help with building out the different choices your participants may make.

It is strongly recommended that you come up with a root cause for whatever disaster your scenario is based on. For example, in a ransomware scenario you may want to build up a root cause for the attack coming through a phishing email that one of the executives clicked on or even a malicious USB stick that a low-level employee found outside the building and plugged into their computer.

This root cause is not something that you would communicate until the end of the tabletop exercise itself, but understanding what it is as you are building out the exercise can definitely help you shape some of the outcomes from decisions that the participants may make.

In the case of our sample scenario, the root cause is an external threat actor trying to get onto the network and is being held back by our MFA solution. They have valid credentials for a user, but the MFA authorization is stopping them from progressing, so they have decided to "spam" the user with notification requests in the hopes of wearing them down to get them to click "Approve," thus allowing them to continue their attack. Their end goal may be to install ransomware, exfiltrate data, or just cause general chaos by deleting a bunch of data. This level of specifics is up for interpretation, so whatever you feel is reasonable would be fine. The point is that our initial scenario is a symptom, not the root cause of what is happening.

Decision Trees and Mind Maps

You've selected a scenario and now you're ready to build out the exercise. Great! What's next? Well, what would you do if you were orchestrating this tabletop exercise with a group of participants? You would start by explaining the scenario and the situation that they find themselves in, and then what? Normally I start things off by asking the question: "What do you want to do next?"

Once you've decided, write this decision down. This is your first step toward building a gamified tabletop exercise! Great job! But what if there are other things you also considered? Well, write those down as well! Now you're introducing multiple decision branches in your tabletop exercise! How very exciting! But wait, won't this get messy? Well, yes it will. And quickly. So, what can you do? This is where the idea of decision trees and mind maps come into play.

Let's see how we can model a tabletop exercise around this with some tools to make our job easier, starting with decision trees.

What's a Decision Tree?

A *decision tree* is a type of flowchart that essentially has nodes that are events, current state of affairs, or questions that need to be answered. The branches from these nodes are the decisions you would make leading to a new situation, state, or outcome. This process repeats itself until you reach a satisfactory conclusion to the initial question, situation, or event.

Decision trees are often used in a variety of fields, including financial, healthcare, computer science, marketing, etc. Figure 4-1 shows a simple example of a decision tree.

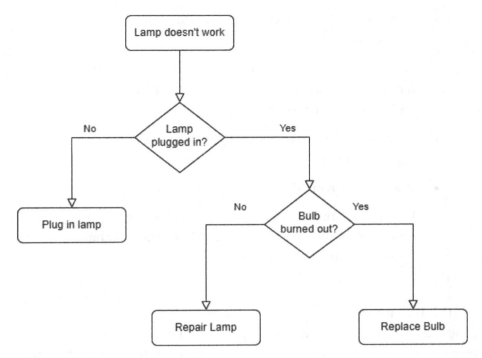

Figure 4-1. *Sample Decision Tree*

As you can see from this sample decision tree, we branch off based on different choices to come to a new state or outcome, where further decisions can be made. This is a great way to start determining the different steps participants can take during the tabletop exercise and is the required first step in preparing for gamification of the exercise itself, but we'll get to those details soon enough. For now, let's focus on this method of planning out possible decisions and their outcomes.

Bringing our attention back to the example scenario above, namely, "*An employee is repeatedly receiving MFA push notifications,*" what would be a possible first step? Here is a short list of what someone may do when faced with a situation like this:

- Confirm that the user didn't invoke this push notification.

- Check the logs on the MFA provider to see where these requests are coming from, i.e., what's the IP address and where is it located?

- Determine if this is a new occurrence or has this happened before?

- Has the user recently changed their password?

- Has the user received any suspicious emails, text messages, or phone calls recently where they may have shared sensitive information?

- Etc.

This is by no means an exhaustive list, and I'm certain that you, my good reader, likely have a few more suggestions. Great! The more the merrier! If you have a playbook or some other process/procedure document to deal with such a situation, then referring to that can help drive the possible decisions to make in this scenario. Now using these possible decisions, let's see what the decision tree would look like (Figure 4-2).

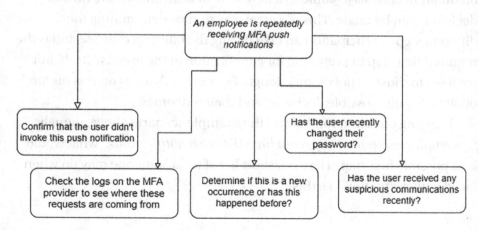

Figure 4-2. *Decision Tree for Sample Scenario*

This is a great way to record ideas and get a nice visual representation of the different decisions that can be made. This can continue with each of these decision nodes to determine the next actions, moving forward until an end state is reached. By using some flowcharting software, you have a much larger canvas to write out the decision tree, which will make it a lot easier to follow during the exercise itself.

But the one question you may have is, what if you yourself aren't sure what to do next? Well, there are a few options here as well:

1. Refer to the disaster recovery and/or business continuity plan, if you have one and it's applicable.

2. Reach out to some subject matter experts (SMEs) for advice on what other options they would recommend.

3. Look for documentation on best practices by scouring the Internet and finding relevant documentation on what may be a viable option. Just be sure not to overshare any sensitive information if you're going to talk to Internet strangers.

A lot of the time, it boils down to personal experience, either your own or from a SME. Here's a secret that you should know if you feel a bit overwhelmed or frustrated:

You do not have to be perfect! You are allowed to miss things!

While you may aim to be as exhaustive and complete in writing out different choices at each step, the reality is that you are going to miss something, and someone is going to decide that you never accounted for. That's okay; it's expected. I've never run a tabletop exercise myself where someone hasn't come up with something I honestly never thought of or anticipated, and that's okay! In a future chapter, we'll go over tips dealing with such situations, but for now just be aware that they can happen and that this should be expected. Use this fact to give yourself some breathing room when coming up with a list of possible decisions the participants may make.

If you're looking for software to help create a decision tree, pretty much any flowchart software will do. There's nothing special about these types of diagrams, but I wouldn't recommend just writing them out on paper as they can get quite large and unruly. Tools like Microsoft Visio, Lucidchart, draw.io, Miro, etc., can all be used to make decision trees.

Some folks may say certain shapes should be used for these types of nodes, etc., but I say just go with what works for you. These types of diagrams are meant to help the conductor or the tabletop exercise with the actual execution; it's not something that will be shared with participants since you do not want to influence their decision-making during the exercise.

You may end up taking part of the flowchart afterward and using it to document your disaster recovery process for the scenario you are testing, but that's about it. Even then, you will likely use a subset of the flowchart based on what you feel works.

Now some of you may look at this flowchart and feel that it's going to be overwhelming and unwieldy as more and more decision nodes are added to it. You're right to have this concern, and it's why I moved away from decision trees and moved to *mind maps* instead. There's no functional difference between the two, but from a layout perspective, I find them easier to follow and work with.

What's a Mind Map?

A *mind map* is another type of diagram, but it is mainly used to organize information in a hierarchy that is centered around a single concept, basically branching outward from a key concept, idea, or state. It's often used by people who are trying to brainstorm around an idea and using the mind map to track the relationships between the ideas they have as they come up with them.

A mind map is not superior to a decision tree, it's just another method for plotting out ideas. Personally, I prefer using mind maps, but functionally they are equivalent to decision trees. At the end of the day, I recommend using whatever method works best for you. Heck, even using a stand-alone document or a spreadsheet full of ideas is fine, if you can organize your thoughts and write out the different ideas you can come up with for the situation at hand.

Let's take a quick look at what a mind map looks like for our sample scenario, using the same possible initial decisions (Figure 4-3).

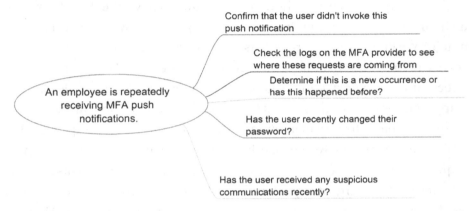

Figure 4-3. *Mind Map for Sample Scenario*

Personally, I find this layout to be a bit easier to follow and work through, but again this is a personal preference. Again, whatever works for you is the right solution, but I do encourage you to try a few different options until you find one that works well for you.

Most of the same software that can help build decision trees can also be used to build mind maps, or you can get some dedicated mind map software. Personally, I am using an open source software package called *Freeplane* to build the mind maps in this book. I will be using mind maps moving forward for the rest of the book, as appropriate.

Building Out the Scenario

Now that we've discussed how we're going to build our scenario, let's go back and determine what's next. We discussed that for a decision tree you want to continue filling out the tree until you've come to some type of end state or conclusion from the original problem. The same idea goes for mind maps as well; you will continue to include new ideas until you reach exhaustion or some end state for your starting point At least when building a gamified tabletop!

The next question is then how do you know when you're done? How far should you go when building out these diagrams? How many levels is enough? We know what the root cause is, so is the plan to build out the exercise to the point that the participants reach the logical conclusion? I'd recommend against going that far, mainly because it's an exercise in disappointment. Why do I say that? Well, from experience for starters!

You may have the best of intentions and think you can come up with all possible steps someone would take, but different people will come up with unique solutions and decisions you may have never considered. This is not a bad thing at all, just the reality at hand. The last thing anyone wants to do is spend hours upon hours working on a diagram mapping out different decisions, only to have 95% of those decisions never come up during the exercise. Less is more when it comes to designing and building out a tabletop exercise.

Start small and simple. Come up with three to six different choices someone can make for a given state, pick one of those branches, and then flesh it out with another three to six choices. Repeat for a maximum of three levels of decision, but don't feel like you need to have many possible decisions for each. For example, sometimes there may only be one logical decision to be made for a given situation, and that's okay! To start, try going no more than three levels deep. With experience, you may go down a bit further, but many times you won't go down more than five to six levels deep in total, and most of the time these final levels don't require preplanning but can be done during the exercise itself.

Rather than continue to talk about this, let us go through our existing scenario and see what this looks like. I'm going to use the mind map version just out of personal preference here. Looking at the list of decisions, the first one is "*Confirm that the user didn't invoke this push notification.*" That's straightforward as the answer is either yes or no. If yes, then obviously the question is why? Perhaps there is a misunderstanding on how the process works, perhaps they experience a lag, etc. The more interesting option is when they say "no," they are not the ones that are triggering these many push notifications. So now the question is what does this look like in our mind map? Figure 4-4 shows what it could look like.

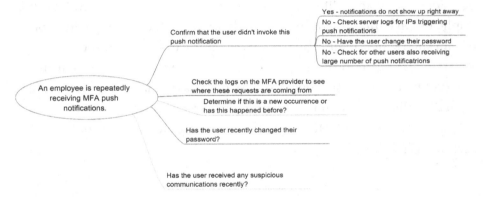

Figure 4-4. *Second-Level Decision Example*

There are two things I want to point out in this mind map. The first is that there is no "intermediate state" between the decision to check with the user if they are clicking the notify button multiple times and then the next decision on what to do with their answer, i.e., there is no "yes" or "no" state. Instead, I used a short prefix for the decisions to note what led to this particular choice. This is strictly personal preference! You absolutely could use another intermediate decision node to indicate the outcome and branch from there, or you could use a different colored line instead, indicating the reason leading to the decision. The point is that there is a lot of flexibility here.

Moving forward, the same process would be done for the remaining initial decisions, then further refining those new decision states with yet another level. Very quickly the diagram will grow, and it will start to feel a bit wild. I recommend not going further than three levels for many of your decisions and generally no more than five levels for those that have predefined steps (such as part of a playbook, existing plan, etc.) to avoid unnecessary complexity to the diagram.

Some of you may notice that there's a repeat in the decision nodes above, specifically around checking the IP address of the requests. This is a common issue that can happen during modeling, namely, a repeat in the decisions available at different states of the exercise. I recommend leaving duplicates like this and just repeating them rather than trying to loop back or join such states, mainly because it makes the diagram harder to follow. When reflecting on the exercise, it can help to identify how you came to a particular decision, so a post-exercise discussion may suggest checking something like this sooner in the process if it was found to be useful.

Let's see what a fully filled-out mind map would look like for this scenario (Figure 4-5).

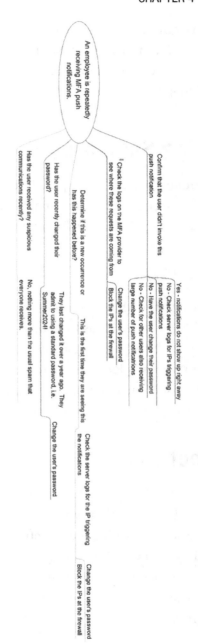

Figure 4-5. *Full Mind Map Example*

This is meant as an example, and obviously there may be more decisions to be made, but for the sake of illustration I'm going to cap the divisions at four levels at the deepest. Hopefully this gives you an idea of what a filled-out mind map may look like.

Tips for Building Scenarios

Alright, so we covered quite a bit, but let me pull things together in a set of tips to help you when starting out with your own tabletops. Before starting to add gamification elements, we need a solid foundation for the exercise itself.

Start with a Scenario

Start with some type of situation that you will use as the basis of the tabletop exercise itself. You can get ideas from discussions with employees, from news headlines, from the @badthingsdaily X/Twitter account, from your own disaster recovery plans, etc. The point is to come up with something that makes sense for your organization and is somewhat possible to actually impact your organization.

Determine a Root Cause

Once you've selected a scenario, try to fill it out by determining what the root cause of the situation is, i.e., if it's a cyber attack, what is the goal of the attackers? This will help you determine the direction you will want to lead the participants in as they start working through the exercise. Remember, they must not know the root cause until the tabletop exercise itself is complete, but you will want to keep it in mind as you work through the planning and design phases.

Plan for Decisions

With a scenario selected, and a root cause in mind, start thinking about some initial decisions that a participant may make when faced with the initial scenario. You can rehearse by outlining the initial scenario/situation and then asking yourself "What do you want to do next?" The answers to that question will be the starting point for the remainder of the exercise.

Start Diagramming

Using either a decision tree or a mind map, use your charting software of choice and start filling out decisions that you expect participants to make at each stage of the exercise. Personally, I mix between filling out all possible initial decisions that the participants may make and going back and doing a deeper dive on each decision by following through the possible outcomes between three and five levels deep, then repeating.

Having repeat decisions at different parts/levels of the chart is fine, as your participants may end up making the same choices at different points in the exercise, so repeats are okay! Try to use any features of your charting software to your advantage, such as adding notes on the decision nodes to give yourself more context or information that you can convey during the exercise.

Try to keep in mind the root cause of the situation that the participants are facing. This may help with this context as well as the different decisions that the participants will make. It's best to reveal information on an as-needed basis and not give too much away.

After each decision, ask yourself the same question: "What do you want to do next?" This will help you come up with the next set of decisions that a participant may make, thus filling out your diagram further.

The initial diagram should be straightforward and simple. Don't go overboard with possible solutions at each stage, and don't feel like you need to go deeper than three to five decisions initially. You can always go back and add additional situations/decisions as you see fit. With experience, you will be able to come up with more possible decisions that the participants will make, so don't feel as if you must fill out the diagram fully.

Use Notes

Depending on the software package you're using, it may have the option to add notes to the decision nodes in your diagram. This is a great way to add additional context you can refer to during the tabletop exercise, such as the state of the environment after a decision is made.

Referring to our example scenario above, you may have a note on the decisions to check the server logs to see what IPs are requesting the push notifications and see that there are a vast majority coming from an Eastern European country, but not the location where the user is located. This additional context may be difficult to capture in the node directly, but absolutely will help with the planning of the exercise.

This one is important, so you will want to find some software that can help you do this before you get to the gamification element, as it will be used in future chapters.

Edit, Revise, and Expand

If you have a technical editor or someone else who can help you review your diagram, please have them review it when you feel you are done. This step is optional, but can be helpful if you are just starting out. Getting that extra perspective can be invaluable.

Just make sure you do not use a future participant to do the review! You want the outline of the exercise to be unknown to those who will participate in it, so initially you want to keep this plan secret. After an iteration, it's fine to ask for feedback and revise it further, but in general you want to pick someone to review who is outside of the potential participant pool.

Repeat this process until you have a solid draft of your tabletop exercise, at least with the initial set of decisions and possible outcomes. Adding in the gamification elements will come next, but we want a solid skeleton in place first.

Summary

This was a big chapter as we started to get into the design of the tabletop exercise itself! Very exciting! There's a lot to digest here, but ultimately it boils down to pacing yourself and working in phases. Start with a scenario, figure out the root cause of the problem, start mapping out what you would do if faced with the same problem, and start planning out these decisions using your favorite charting software, creating a decision tree or mind map. Go through a few revisions until you are satisfied that you have a good outline for your tabletop exercise.

In the next chapter, we will look at gamification elements, what they are, how they work, and how and when to incorporate them into your design. We will continue with the same example scenario just to keep things consistent. Now the real games (no pun intended) begin.

CHAPTER 5

Adding Randomness

Up to this point, we have walked through the steps to build a successful tabletop exercise for an organization. The problem that we still face, and one of the main reasons I came up with the idea behind gamifying tabletop exercises, is the problem of the *happy path*. This is the term I use to describe a participant group working through a tabletop exercise without any issue or problem occurring during the exercise.

Is the happy path unobtainable? Absolutely not, but as I'm sure most of you will agree with the fact that when a crisis erupts, things hardly go according to plan. You may have contingencies in place for when unexpected situations arise, but my point is that these unexpected situations are rarely ever raised during a traditional tabletop exercise. This leads to boredom, overconfidence, and generally apathy toward disaster recovery planning among the participants of the exercise, which defeats the purpose of the exercise.

Introducing Alternative Outcomes

The question then becomes, how do we avoid this "happy path" problem? Well, we can inject some random outcomes into the decision process, namely, if a participant makes a decision, we can just state that it was wrong and provide a consequence as necessary. The problem here is that this is an arbitrary decision made by the conductor. If it's arbitrary, the

© John Svazic 2025
J. Svazic, *Gamified Tabletop Exercises for Effective Disaster Recovery Testing*,
https://doi.org/10.1007/979-8-8688-1252-1_5

55

participant(s) may view this as biased and the individual being targeted due to some perceived feud/issue with the conductor and the participant. We clearly want to avoid this bias, so we need something else to introduce this randomness that removes the conductor from the equation as much as possible.

Rolling the Dice

Dice are a great mechanism for introducing randomness as their outcome is (normally) not predictable. As such, they are a great way to introduce randomness to a decision while providing the illusion of control with the person who is rolling them. This way, no other person, be it the conductor or another participant, can be accused of undue influence or bias for the outcome.

Now that we have a non-biased method for introducing randomness for the potential consequences for a decision made during the tabletop exercise, the next question to ask is *which die should we be rolling*? To answer that question, we should first establish some general rules around potential consequences.

Outcomes of Decisions

To avoid the "happy path," not every decision can be the correct one. What does that mean? Well, to put it simply, sometimes a decision made by a participant will not work out in some way. For example, if the situation is that access to the Internet was interrupted, a participant may decide to check the router, only to find that it is not functioning. They may decide that the best course of action is to unplug it, wait 30 seconds, and plug it in again. The happy path would be that this decision would work as this is a known problem with this router, but the decision to replace it has been postponed because this solution has always worked.

But what would happen if this solution failed? Sounds like a great candidate for a consequence! So, what would a potential consequence be? There are so many options! It's best to consider three consequences for any decision, namely, a bad, average, and good consequence for the decision. This makes coming up with consequences easier. In some situations, there may only be two consequences, good or bad, but we'll get into those edge cases later in the chapter.

So going back to the example, if the participant decides that they want to unplug the router, wait 30 seconds, and then plug it back in to fix the issue, then here are three possible outcomes (worst, average, and best, respectively):

1.   The router sparks as you try to plug it back in, and there's a distinct smell of burning electronics coming from the device with a small amount of smoke.

2.   You plug the router back in without incident, but Internet access is still not available.

3.   The reset procedure worked as expected, and Internet access has been restored.

So now that we have the possible outcomes for a decision, the next step is to determine which one will be selected. This is where we need to consider some basic math, specifically *probabilities*.

Probabilities

A *probability* is the likelihood that something will happen, often measured as a percentage. So when we're talking about the different outcomes from a decision, the probability of one of those decisions happening just means the measure of how likely it is for that outcome to happen.

Sometimes when we define outcomes, we want each of them to be equally viable, meaning that they will all have the same probability of occurring. Other times we may want certain outcomes to be less likely, such as a worst- or best-case outcome, as they may take the tabletop exercise in a different direction than expected by the participants, which may be undesirable depending on the situation. Being able to determine this likelihood ahead of time can be quite useful.

With that definition out of the way, let's see how the idea of probabilities translates into rolling dice in our gamified tabletops and how we can take advantage of this.

Controlling Outcomes with Dice

Types of Dice

For the remainder of the book, we will be discussing the use of dice to introduce the random element to gamified tabletops, but specifically we are going to talk about two different types of dice used. Most of us are familiar with the "standard" six-sided die, i.e., dice with six sides, numbered one through six. We will refer to one of these dice as a 1D6, i.e., a single six-sided die.

In addition to the single 6-sided die, we will also introduce the less common 20-sided die, which as you may have guessed includes the numbers 1 through 20 and is most associated with tabletop games such as *Dungeons and Dragons* (*D&D*). This style of dice is easily obtainable online or from a local game shop that sells tabletop games such as *D&D*, *Warhammer 40k*, etc. They can be bought individually or in a set of other uncommon dice, but we will only focus on the 20-sided die. As with the 6-sided die, we will refer to this as a 1D20, indicating a single 20-sided die.

Sometimes having physical access to dice is not possible, especially if doing a tabletop exercise with remote participants, as not everyone will have physical dice available to them. Not a problem! There are many online dice rollers available. A quick online search will help you find one. I personally am a fan of the dice roller that Google provides when you search for "dice roller" as you can specify the number and type of dice you want to roll, i.e., a 1D6 or 1D20, all from within your web browser.

Now with our 1D6 and 1D20 in (virtual) hands, we can start looking into when to use which die for determining outcomes of a decision by the participants.

When to Use Which Die?

When should you use a 1D6 versus a 1D20? Well, as all good consultant answers start with, *it depends*. Let's go back to our Internet outage example from earlier. If we know that the participant is going to say they want to unplug the router to power cycle it to reset it, there are three possible outcomes of this decision:

1. The router sparks as you try to plug it back in, and there's a distinct smell of burning electronics coming from the device with a small amount of smoke.

2. You plug the router back in without incident, but Internet access is still not available.

3. The reset procedure worked as expected, and Internet access has been restored.

The first outcome is the worst-case scenario, the second outcome is the average-case scenario, and the third outcome is the best-case scenario. If we wanted to treat each of them as equal possibilities, we could use either a 1D6 or a 1D20, but a 1D6 would be easier. Why? Because there are three possible outcomes, and the 1D6 has six possible values. Six divided by three is two, meaning that we could assign the outcome of a roll of a 1D6 as shown in Table 5-1.

Table 5-1. *1D6 Roll Outcomes*

Die Roll Shows	Outcome Scenario	Probability
1	1 (Worst)	~33.333%
2	1 (Worst)	
3	2 (Average)	~33.333%
4	2 (Average)	
5	3 (Best)	~33.333%
6	3 (Best)	

You may notice that I'm using lower values to map to the less desirable outcomes. This is consistent with how most tabletop games work, namely, the lower the value of the roll, the less desirable the outcome of the dice roll. We will continue this trend with the gamified tabletops for the rest of the book.

As we can see in the table, there is about a 1-in-3 chance for any of these outcomes to occur, i.e., each one has two possible values of the dice roll to be possible, or just over a 33% chance of occurring. This may be sufficient for most possible outcomes, but what if we wanted to exercise a bit more control? What if we know that a standard reset process will not work in this scenario, or is not something we want to trigger most of the time? This type of fine-tuning of the probabilities is where *roulette wheel* selection comes into play.

Roulette Wheel Selection

What exactly is *roulette wheel selection*? It is a method by which we can control the probability for a given outcome by selecting a wider or narrower range of values to ensure a greater or lesser probability for a given outcome. Think of a wheel that is broken up into individual sections, just like a roulette wheel. But rather than every section being of equal size, some of them will be larger, while others will be smaller, like a pie chart. The larger segments represent the more likely outcome we want to occur, while the smaller sections represent the less probable outcomes.

Bringing this back to our previous example, let's assume that we think that it's most likely that restarting the router by unplugging it is not going to work, so we would like this to be the more likely scenario to occur. Using the 1D6 chart above, all three outcomes have the same probability of occurring, namely, around 33%, or 1-in-3 for each scenario. What if we used a 1D20 instead? Well, it won't be equal right off the bat because you can't easily break the three scenarios equally across the 20 values of the 1D20, which means that at least one scenario will be less likely to occur, at least statistically.

But what if this is exactly what we want? Let's put together another table (Table 5-2), this time using a 1D20, to showcase how we would want to make outcome 2 more likely than outcomes 1 or 3, by increasing its probability.

Table 5-2. *1D20 Roll Outcomes*

Die Roll Shows	Outcome Scenario	Probability
1	1 (Worst)	10%
2	1 (Worst)	
3	2 (Average)	80%
4	2 (Average)	
5	2 (Average)	
6	2 (Average)	
7	2 (Average)	
8	2 (Average)	
9	2 (Average)	
10	2 (Average)	
11	2 (Average)	
12	2 (Average)	
13	2 (Average)	
14	2 (Average)	
15	2 (Average)	
16	2 (Average)	
17	2 (Average)	
18	2 (Average)	
19	3 (Best)	10%
20	3 (Best)	

Things are a bit different this time around, don't you think? We're essentially giving more "weight" to outcome 2, namely, that the power cycle process does not work for the router, but it is not completely broken either. However, there is still a smaller probability that either the router short-circuits (outcome 1) or it resets successfully (outcome 3). The catch is that there is only a 10% chance that either of these will work. We could further limit the probability of outcome 3 by reducing it to a 5% probability by only allowing a roll of 20 to trigger that outcome, which for those who have played traditional tabletop games in the past will know is rare to see. This is what we mean by talking about roulette wheel selection, but in this case the "house" is cheating by controlling the probabilities by changing the size of each section on the wheel.

Breaking Down Probabilities

When we use a 1D6, each value of the die represents a 1-in-6 probability of that value occurring, or roughly a 16.67% chance of occurring. Grouping two digits, such as rolling a 1 *or* 2 for a scenario, gives us a 33.33% probability. Combining three digits (i.e., 1, 2, *or* 3) gives us a 50% probability, and so forth. Here's another quick table (Table 5-3) outlining the probabilities for different ranges using a 1D6.

Table 5-3. *1D6 Outcome Probability Breakdown*

Number of Values per Outcome	Probability (Percentage)
1	~16.67%
2	~33.34%
3	50%
4	~66.67%
5	~83.34%

Obviously, if all six values were tied to a single outcome, then you would have a 100% probability of that outcome occurring, so we're leaving that off the chart. Now let's draw up the same chart for a 1D20 (Table 5-4).

Table 5-4. *1D20 Outcome Probability Breakdown*

Number of Values per Outcome	Probability (Percentage)
1	5%
2	10%
3	15%
4	20%
5	25%
6	30%
7	35%
8	40%
9	45%
10	50%
11	55%
12	60%
13	65%
14	70%
15	75%
16	80%
17	85%
18	90%
19	95%

Again, assigning all 20 values to a single outcome would result in a 100% probability of that outcome occurring, but that doesn't really help when we're trying to differentiate between outcomes.

Recommendations for Dice Rolling

The beauty of the 1D20 is the more fine-grained control that you can achieve when using this idea of roulette wheel selection. We can more easily control the probability of a given outcome compared to others by providing that outcome with a larger "section" of possible dice roll values. Because of this fact, I tend to use a 1D20 when I want to give more "weight" to a particular outcome, while I will use a 1D6 when the probability of the different outcomes is more or less the same, or I'm okay with a wider likelihood for one scenario versus the others, i.e., ~66.67% for one scenario, but ~16.677% for the other two.

Here are some general rules I personally use when determining which type of die to use when rolling for different outcomes:

- Use a 1D6 when the probability between outcomes is nearly equal.

- Use a 1D20 if you want to give an advantage to one or two outcomes versus the other, or two of the scenarios should be unlikely to occur, i.e., best- and worst-case outcomes for a decision.

- The more subtle you want to be with the probabilities between outcomes, the more reason to go with a 1D20.

- When in doubt, keep it simple and stick with the 1D6 as it is more familiar and fairer.

- The 1D20 will feel exotic and may be a fan favorite, but varying the use of the 1D6 and 1D20 will keep the participants engaged.

Consider these guidelines rather than hard-and-fast rules. As you design and run your gamified tabletop exercises, you will get a sense for what feels more natural. But this does lead to some other guidelines to consider when adding in this sense of randomness to the tabletop exercise.

Guidelines for Dice Rolling Outcomes

With the addition of a dice rolling mechanic to provide various outcomes from decisions, it is very tempting to use them for every decision, but you should resist this temptation. First off, the novelty wears out quickly, and it will slow down the overall execution of the exercise itself. If every decision needs a dice roll, participants will quickly become bored and irritated as no decision can possibly be made that is considered correct if everything is left to chance.

Instead, I would recommend starting with adding the dice rolling mechanic to maybe 25–40% of all mapped out decisions within your tabletop exercise to start. This doesn't have to be an exact number, and it may be smaller initially. Try to identify decisions that may have multiple outcomes, perhaps a best- and worst-case scenario, and start with those. Try to avoid more than two to three decisions in a row that require a dice roll if you can avoid it.

Remember, not everything goes according to plan during an incident. Even the best laid plans are subject to change, so that's what we want to replicate here. Just enough to warrant not falling down the trap of the "happy path" and leading everyone to a false sense of preparedness.

When coming up with possible outcomes for a decision, try to ensure no more than two to three possible outcomes are determined. There may be countless outcomes for some situations, but as we mentioned earlier, try to go with a worst-, average-, and best-case scenario. Sometimes even a worse- and best-case scenario is all you need.

If there is no need for different outcomes for a decision, then don't try to force any! This is the default after all, since not every decision will have different outcomes. Again, sticking to a 40% rule for the number of decisions that may have multiple outcomes will help keep you on track, so identifying which decisions are just going to have a fixed outcome can be another way for you to help identify which decisions should be candidates for dice rolling due to multiple outcomes associated with them.

Now that we've discussed quite a bit about outcomes and how rolling dice can help you determine which outcome will occur, let's revisit our planning document and see how we can add this mechanic to our tabletop exercise diagram.

Adding Gamification to Mind Maps

For this section, we will revisit the mind map we used in the last chapter, where an employee repeatedly received MFA push notifications asking to confirm their identity (Figure 5-1).

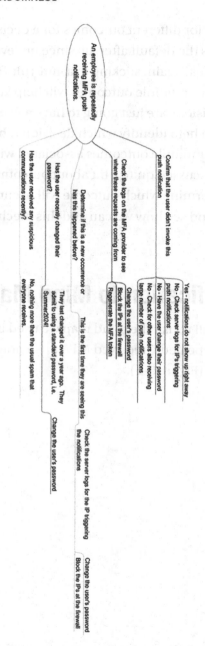

Figure 5-1. *Mind Map for Push Notification Flooding*

This is a good first step in building out our gamified tabletop, so now let's see how to start adding those gamified elements. A few things to keep in mind:

- We don't want to go overboard with the dice rolling, so maybe 20–30% of the decisions will involve a dice roll.

- When we introduce a dice roll for the outcome, for simple/equally probable outcomes, we will use a 1D6; for more weighted or complex probabilities, we will use a 1D20 for the rolls.

- Start reviewing the mind map from the earliest decisions/outcomes to determine if something downstream may change.

With these points in mind, let's get started! Starting with the first outcome that the participants may choose to do, namely, *Confirm that the user didn't invoke this push notification*, this seems like a great candidate for a dice roll. If we look at the subsequent branches, there are two distinct possibilities; either the user did initiate the login procedure, or they did not. The other outcomes are based on one of those two possibilities. Since there are only two possibilities, a simple 1D6 roll should suffice.

Using a 1D6, we can split the decisions into rolling one to three results in an answer of "No," or a four to six would represent a "Yes" answer from the user. We can then base the next decisions from one of those outcomes.

The first step is to update the decision node to indicate that a roll will be required, so I will update the title to read "Confirm that the user didn't invoke this push notification (Roll 1D6)." You could also change the node color, size, font, etc., if you desire, but I like to keep things simple.

Next, I will use the notes feature of the node to add a description for the dice roll outcomes, along with any additional context for the outcomes. In this case, if the result is "Yes," then there is some additional context that the user experiences some delay between requesting a push notification and the push notification coming through to their device. Rather than using another node in the mind map to display this information, I will move it to the notes section for this specific outcome. The other decisions that can be made if the answer is instead "No" will remain as decision nodes in the mind map, since they are possible next steps that the participants will take.

No other decision nodes will be added as this seems sufficient for now. Of course you are always welcome to add more, but just focus on the decisions themselves rather than adding more dice rolling at this point. Our focus for gamification is just on these initial decision nodes now.

Figure 5-2 shows what this would look like after updating the mind map. Note that I've minimized the other branches as we are focused on this branch for now.

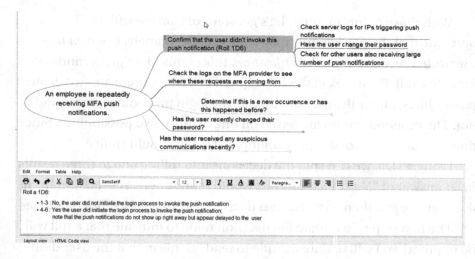

Figure 5-2. *Adding a Gamified Decision Node*

Moving on to the other decision nodes from the main node, all the other decision nodes are candidates. But going back to our rule of trying to be sparing with the dice rolling, we'll only pick one more to add the dice rolling mechanic to. I will arbitrarily decide on the last decision node, namely, *Has the user received any suspicious communications recently?*

This is an interesting choice because as the mind map is designed so far, it only has the one possible outcome, but I'd like to revisit and add some more possibilities here. I think this question has at least three possible outcomes; a best-case scenario, a worst-case scenario, and an average-case scenario. Let's start by determining what these scenarios look like:

- *Best-case scenario*: No suspicious emails outside of the standard spam that goes to the spam folder, which are ignored.

- *Average-case scenario*: Some suspicious emails arrived, but the user had marked them as spam after reviewing the emails.

- *Worst-case scenario*: There was a weird email containing a link for an invoice that they clicked on. They did try to log in to see the document, but it didn't seem to work and constantly complained about an invalid password.

Now that we have the three scenarios written out, it's time to decide how to split up the possibilities. Since we want to test a disaster scenario, we are going to put more weight on the worst-case scenario and less weight on the other two scenarios. I'm going to go with a 25%, 25%, 50% weighting for the best-, average-, and worst-case scenarios, respectively, which translates to the following dice roll outcomes:

- Roll 1–10: Worst-case scenario

- Roll 11–15: Average-case scenario

- Roll 16–20: Best-case scenario

Once again, we're using the convention that the worst outcomes are associated with the lower dice values, while the best outcomes are associated with the highest values. Since we're using a 20-sided die, each digit represents a 5% probability of occurring; thus, a range of ten values gives us a 50% probability of that outcome, while a range of five values gives us a 25% probability of that outcome occurring. This gives us the breakdown of the rolls above.

Now with the rolls determined, we can revisit the subsequent decision nodes to determine if we need to update any of them, remove any, or add new ones. Clearly, we do as there are no logical next steps listed in our original map, so we'll add some new decisions. Note that we're only adding new decision nodes, not looking to add any dice rolling to those at this point.

After updating the mind map, we have the diagram shown in Figure 5-3.

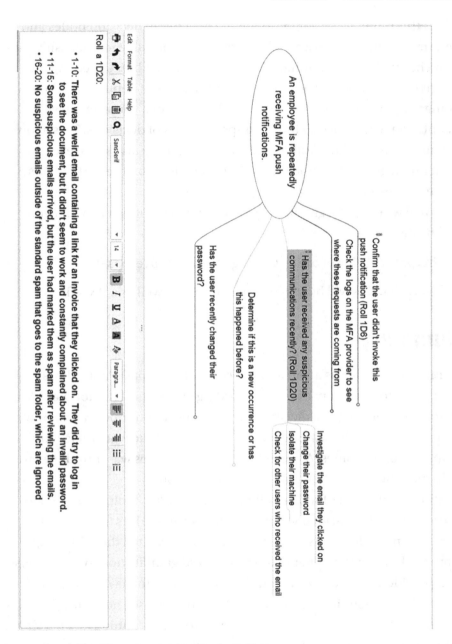

Figure 5-3. *Further Decision Node Editing*

At this point, we can move on to the next tier of decision nodes and determine which of those would be candidates for dice rolling, using these same heuristics to determine which ones would be best suited. Again, I want to stress that you want to go breadth first, not depth first, when doing the gamification steps. By going breadth first, you won't have the temptation to add dice rolling on a specific path of decisions. This allows you to balance the dice rolling mechanic a bit more across the exercise, rather than giving the appearance that every decision the participants make will result in a dice roll.

We'll wrap up the gamification work at this point, but a full diagram will be made available at

```
https://github.com/jsvazic/gamified-tabletops-book
```

Note that this will be in Freeplane format as well as a PNG file.

Summary

Gamification helps us avoid the trap of the "happy path" and allows reusability to a tabletop exercise by adding elements of randomness. We introduced the idea of a dice rolling mechanic to introduce randomness to decisions, but also introduced the idea of "roulette wheel selection" to help control outcomes. A breakdown of probabilities was introduced to help map these out when planning your dice rolls.

Some quick rules for dice rolling were included, including when to use which die (a six-sided versus a twenty-sided die), as well as not to have too many decisions left to a dice roll. We revisited the mind map from the last chapter to figure out how to add gamification to the exercise and provided some advice to limit the dice rolling to maybe 25–40% of the decisions resulting in a dice roll. We also discussed going breadth first when it comes to reviewing the mind map to avoid running down a single line of decisions and only adding gamification to those decisions, which is important to balance the exercise out for the participants.

In the next chapter, we are going to look at tackling the unknown – what to do when you're faced with a decision from the participants that you did not anticipate, or some new information is introduced by the participants that you were not aware of when the tabletop exercise was designed.

CHAPTER 6

Preparing for the Unknown

The irony of running a tabletop exercise, let alone one designed to introduce randomness and variable outcomes based on decisions, is that the exercise itself is full of unknowns. From scheduling conflicts to plans not being followed, to new information being introduced during the exercise, to participants making a decision that wasn't accounted for as part of the planning of the exercise, there will always be some sort of hurdle to overcome. In this chapter, we will look at some of these potential roadblocks and provide some strategies to deal with them to avoid derailing the entire exercise.

Conductor's Temperament

Before we go into different issues you may run into from participants, let's have a quick refresher for the conductor's role and their temperament related to the exercise itself. The purpose of the conductor is to provide an understanding of the state of the disaster at any point during the exercise, but not to introduce their own opinions on what should be done next or what they had missed. Even the root cause is often withheld until the end of the exercise.

© John Svazic 2025
J. Svazic, *Gamified Tabletop Exercises for Effective Disaster Recovery Testing*,
https://doi.org/10.1007/979-8-8688-1252-1_6

The conductor should remain a neutral party and not attempt to influence the decisions of any of the participants. This can be hard, especially if the conductor wants to help, but their purpose during a tabletop exercise is to provide information and let the participants make their own decisions.

The conductor should step in when participants are breaking the original rules for the tabletop exercise, such as questioning the purpose of the exercise, being rude or abusive toward other participants, or making the exercise itself ineffective through their actions.

Let's look at some of the common archetypes of problematic participants that you may encounter during a tabletop exercise.

Problematic Participants

When it comes to the people who are participating in the tabletop exercise, oftentimes you will see a mix of personalities emerge. There will be those participants who are shy and timid and those who will try to bully their way through and take charge of everything. So what should you do if you're the conductor for the tabletop exercise?

"Take Charge" Participants

Some participants that take charge and want to lead any incident handling may be the best suited for such a role, but sometimes they "think" that they are. I find that in such situations it is best to let them continue on their own. There are normally a few different outcomes:

- The other participants will call them out on their behavior, pointing out that they are either not qualified or are derailing recovery efforts.

- They will back themselves into a corner and make poor decisions, resulting in a rather unfortunate outcome.

- They are indeed well suited for this leadership role and may end up saving the day!

The only point at which you want to get involved is when they start to harass or alienate the other participants. If you find other participants are tuning out of the exercise, it may be useful to take a break and speak with people individually to try to get them to reengage or even back off to let others take charge.

During the postmortem, it may be useful to point out that overreliance on a single individual may not be in the company's best interest, and thus having a backup may be a good idea. What if this individual isn't available? What if they are no longer with the company? Identifying such pitfalls is another great outcome of a tabletop exercise.

One approach a conductor can take is to let things play out as they are happening and use the postmortem to identify potential issues. It is vital to keep in mind that the point of a tabletop exercise is to practice what would happen in case of a disaster and the team needed to act to recover. If there are personality conflicts, then this is the best time to have them come to light.

Another approach is to remain calm and to remind the participants that this is a simulation and that while passion is a great trait to have, it can be toned down a bit for the given situation, assuming someone is being a bit too aggressive.

Uninterested Participants

Participants who do not want to be there are common. Perhaps they were forced to attend by their boss or are considered "vital" even if they do not agree. While everyone should try to be an active participant, there will almost always be an individual or two who are not involved.

If you know what their role within the organization is, then it may be a matter of a situation that requires their help has not come about yet. This is common with participants from HR and other nontechnology-focused groups. Their participation may be required, but not often and perhaps only once. Some strategies to increase their involvement may include

- Asking questions to the group, seeking insight or recommendations if another participant isn't sure what to do next

- Explicitly calling on them to help with a situation that has arisen, i.e., questions from employees on a given issue if the participant is from HR

If they are being disruptive or having an overall negative impact on the exercise, then excusing them from the exercise may be the right call. If they are needed, they can be called back at a future time. This is a more drastic option and not something I would recommend. Postmortem discussions may be a more appropriate time to discuss these types of observations, so as not to damage the morale of the team during the exercise itself.

One approach, while slightly more complicated, would be to have noncritical participants be on "standby" and called upon when they are needed. The drawback is that they will not have a fixed schedule and may be distracted by other work while they wait for a potential call, but this is a more realistic reflection on what would happen during an actual emergency as not everyone is immediately ready or fully informed of what has been done prior to the call.

"Bully" Participants

Different from the "Take Charge" participant, this type of tabletop participant will try to intimidate or belittle other participants if they try to decide that they do not agree with. This may come from an intense discussion to just overriding their decision and saying that a different approach will be used instead. This is often coming from someone higher in the reporting structure overriding a subordinate, which is common with leaders who do not like having their authority questioned or honestly believe that they are making the correct decision.

The conductor may decide to go with the original decision and let the exercise continue, but these types of negative participants should be discussed (possibly privately with their leaders) after the exercise.

Inquisitive Participants

Participants who want to question everything that is going on are common. Oftentimes, they will be looking for more information than what was provided to determine what the root cause of an issue was, what the appropriate solution should be, why something did not work the way it was supposed to, etc.

While asking questions should be encouraged, it can become disruptive if it is constant and interrupts the flow of the exercise. One approach you can take is to remind them that the facts have been discussed and that no additional information is available now, or if necessary, remind them of a previously stated fact. But also remind them that the disaster is ongoing and that distractions are potentially wasting time as now is not the time to start an introspection.

Offer to table these questions for further discussion during the postmortem but emphasize that trying to figure out what to do during an emergency is not the best way to handle said emergency. For example, questioning why a certain technology failed before dealing with the fallout of the failure is not an appropriate action and may distract from the task at hand. The conductor may allow the discussion, but there should be a consequence for the delay.

If these types of participants start questioning whether the scenario at large is realistic, it's best to remind everyone that the purpose of the exercise is to practice responding to a disaster to continue business operations. I don't know of many disasters that are planned of time, so the root cause can be wildly illogical, but still potentially happen. Again, the focus of the exercise should be on resolving the issue and resuming normal business operations.

Dealing with Problematic Participants

There are some common techniques that you can use to help keep problematic participants in check and on track. First and foremost, try to keep everyone focused on the task at hand, outlining and reminding them of the current situation and whatever decisions have been made up to this point. Sometimes a reset of expectations can help reset potential issues.

Having open communications is key as well. Make sure that people are being heard and share questions that some of these participants make with the wider group to see if additional information may be helpful.

Another approach is to take a break, especially if tempers are starting to flare among the participants. A quick ten-minute break may be sufficient to reset tensions or at least give you an opportunity to speak privately with a troublesome participant or their leader if warranted.

Redirecting conversations that may be derailing the conversation or focus of the participants is also a strategy that you can use. While exploring other options can be beneficial, reminding the participants that time is ticking away and that other consequences may occur if they do not get back on track can help. A great example of this is when participants may be stuck in the small details of a process or procedure but are missing a major activity such as updating key stakeholders.

Introducing unexpected events due to inactivity may help bring attention to these "rabbit hole" discussions; just be sure not to make them too extreme. For example, if the participants have failed to communicate with stakeholders even after a gentle nudge from the conductor, then informing the participants that the stakeholders have made a potentially false statement to internal staff that leads to some headaches because additional time and resources are now required to clear up the misunderstanding. This is a minor inconvenience but illustrates why staying on task is important. I would also recommend bringing up these types of distractions during the postmortem exercise to emphasize the importance of having documented and well-understood procedures in place to avoid these "discovery" discussions that may lead to unintended consequences.

One final approach that you can take, albeit the most extreme, is to simply recommend bringing the exercise to a premature end as there is little progress being made, and it is unlikely that you will be able to achieve the desired results. This is the nuclear option and should only be used if you have multiple difficult participants and are prepared to have a separate discussion with those in charge about the challenges you are facing. This should only be considered as a last resort, as it does undermine the purpose of the tabletop exercise and your own capabilities as a conductor in running an exercise. However, if you have factual evidence of the issues, it may be the only option. After all, it's better to understand the potential problems the team will face in a controlled situation rather than an actual emergency.

Handling Unexpected Decisions

I'll be honest with you, I have yet to host a gamified tabletop exercise where one of the participants hasn't raised a question or performed an action that was unexpected and unaccounted for. This could be due to them having insider information that no one else knew ahead of time or just a decision that wasn't considered during the planning process. Panic naturally ensues, so the question becomes *what do you do next*?

There are a few strategies that you can use to help in situations like this. Some take practice, some take experience, but there are solutions that you can use to avoid derailing the exercise:

- Come up with a potential outcome on the fly.

- Ask the participant what they expect the outcome to be, and either accept this as the valid outcome or provide an alternative that makes sense.

- Ask other participants for potential outcomes and associate those with a dice roll.

- If the decision isn't material, simply provide a neutral outcome that doesn't deter from the main objectives or deter from your own plan.

I'd only recommend performing on-the-fly outcomes if you have experience with the decision made by the participant, as it can again derail the exercise if you misunderstand what the potential outcomes could be.

Asking for input from the other participants is a great strategy as it may lead to other discussions these other folks may not have considered or known about. This usually leads to an update to existing documentation for processes, policies, and/or procedures for the company. Be sure to note these and revisit during any postmortem activities.

The most important thing to remember is to not panic. These unknowns are not unexpected and just need to be dealt with. Sometimes the conductor doesn't have to act at all as one of the other participants may object to the original unexpected decision due to it not being viable, incorrect, etc. What you want to avoid as a conductor is to try to pretend that you understand the unexpected decision and just roll with it. When in doubt, ask for input from the other participants. There's nothing wrong with certain decisions to "just work," as this may be the best-case scenario. Take this as a lesson learned, make a note of it, and update the mind map accordingly.

Uncovering new knowledge and potential unexpected decisions is beneficial as these are often nuggets of knowledge that individual participants may have and not think relevant or believe to be common knowledge, when as quite helpful and not understood by others within the company. Drawing out these facts is another positive outcome of a tabletop exercise and as such should be celebrated and complemented during a postmortem if it was proven to be useful.

Summary

In traditional tabletop exercises, there are not many opportunities for disagreements or friction to occur. However, by adding elements of randomness, this friction increases, and there may be a possibility for unexpected events and/or actions to occur during the tabletop exercise itself.

In this chapter, we examined some of the friction points that may be encountered during these types of exercises, including difficulty with participants and facing unexpected decisions that were not anticipated originally. Strategies to address both were provided, but the first step is to ensure that the conductor has their own temperament in check. It is important that the conductor stay as neutral as possible and not lead the participants down a particular path or set of decisions. Being as neutral as possible can help when dealing with unknown situations as it is clear there is no favoritism among the participants.

In the next chapter, we will look at pulling all these tools and techniques together in order to help with your gamified tabletop exercise design journey.

CHAPTER 7

Running a Gamified Tabletop Exercise

Over the past few chapters, we've covered all the main aspects of gamified tabletop exercises, from generic tabletop exercise processes to how to add randomness via a gamified mechanic using dice rolling. We also looked at how to handle issues and unknowns from participants during the exercise itself. In this chapter, we're going to pull everything together and give you a road map to conduct a gamified tabletop exercise to the best of your ability. Let's get started.

Before You Begin

Prior to hosting the tabletop exercise itself, make sure the following tasks/items are complete:

- An "end state" has been defined for the exercise.

- The tabletop exercise has been planned out.

- Appropriate participants have been invited.

- An outline of the exercise has been defined and communicated.

© John Svazic 2025
J. Svazic, *Gamified Tabletop Exercises for Effective Disaster Recovery Testing*,
https://doi.org/10.1007/979-8-8688-1252-1_7

- The tabletop exercise has been appropriately scheduled.

- Define an "end state" for the exercise.

Let's dive into the details for each of these tasks in more detail.

An "End State" Has Been Defined for the Exercise

When planning for a tabletop exercise, it is important to understand when to call a situation "complete" or "resolved." This may be after restoring operations to a bare minimum capacity, when key services are restored, or even once the root cause analysis has been completed. Defining this end state prior to starting the exercise will be helpful in determining how long the tabletop exercise may take to complete. I would recommend ensuring that this "end goal" is defined prior to planning the exercise itself, as it will help you identify when to consider the exercise complete. This can also help determine how far you need to plan in terms of potential outcomes and decisions that the participants will face and make, respectively.

The Tabletop Exercise Has Been Planned Out

This one is self-explanatory. Essentially, you want to make sure that you have the tabletop exercise planned out to the best of your ability. This could be a decision tree or mind map, but if it has been planned out to the best of your ability, you should be ready. We've discussed some techniques that you can use when facing an unknown outcome or decision from the participants, but the more you can plan ahead of time, the better for the overall execution of the exercise itself.

Things to keep in mind when building out the potential decisions:

- Review any existing disaster recovery or business continuity plans for potential decisions from the participants (if available).

- Speak with experts in different areas to understand what potential decisions could be made in different situations, as well as potential outcomes of those decisions.

  - This is particularly useful when adding different possible outcomes to a decision via a dice roll.

- Perform your own research to see what decisions are most appropriate for a given situation, and plan accordingly.

- Only plan out about two to three decision branches from a particular outcome so as not to overwhelm yourself with potential decisions.

- Overall, plan for about five to seven levels deep with possible outcomes in your mind map or decision tree. This is just a rough heuristic and not a hard-and-fast rule. Some scenarios will require more levels, while others may be on the shorter side. Use your best judgment so that you don't overplan the exercise and have it exceeded your allotted time.

Appropriate Participants Have Been Invited

When planning for a tabletop exercise, it is important to ensure that you have the right participants invited. This is normally a group of individuals that represent the groups that would be involved in the given disaster scenario you are simulating. Sometimes however, you end up including people who are interested in the process, but are not normally active participants during an emergency unless absolutely necessary. Senior leaders often fall into this category, but again it will depend on the organization. There is a difference between involving senior leaders in a decision-making process and having them participate in a set of actions, activities, and implementations that they are too far removed from.

Oftentimes, the goal in an exercise is to establish well-defined lines of communication with these leaders so they can provide input at key moments, all while being kept aware of the situation if they are not actively participating. Simulating this need may be a goal in your tabletop exercise, so just be sure to plan accordingly. After all, the point of the exercise is to practice what should be done during an emergency in a controlled environment, rather than figuring it out during an actual emergency.

Ensure that people invited to the tabletop exercise have a reason to be there, not just because they feel they should be invited or that they would like to understand the process. Providing recordings or inviting them to the postmortem exercise may be a better option. Even offering to invite them "on demand" is a great strategy as this may be more realistic in terms of their involvement during an actual emergency.

An Outline of the Exercise Has Been Defined and Communicated

When it comes to tabletop exercises, not every participant will be aware of what is expected of them or even how the exercise will be run. This is even more true for gamified tabletops! Be sure to have a brief introduction prepared prior to starting the exercise explaining the purpose of the exercise; any mechanics that will be used, i.e., dice rolling; and the rules for participants as we discussed in an earlier chapter. Also, I'd recommend outlining any planned breaks, so that the participants realize this is not going to be a marathon meeting.

By helping the participants understand why they are there, what's expected of them, and how things are supposed to work, they will be more comfortable and generally better engaged with the rest of the exercise.

The Tabletop Exercise Has Been Appropriately Scheduled

For most tabletop exercises, they will take anywhere between two and four hours to "complete" but may take longer depending on the severity of the emergency being simulated. The last thing you want to do is book an eight-hour meeting for these exercises. Likewise, you don't want to underbook and think that a one-hour meeting will suffice.

If time constraints are an issue, i.e., it's impossible to get a four-hour block booked for everyone, then break it up into multiple meetings, perhaps two hours each, but try to keep these meetings as close as possible to one another. If you take a month between meetings, then the start of the next meeting will mostly be spent recapping what was already discussed and may lead to further meetings taking place. The job of the scribe is going to be vital in these cases, as meticulous note taking will help keep everyone on track at the start of any follow-up meetings.

Be generous with the time you allocate for tabletop exercises, but also don't be afraid to cut them short if you reach a satisfactory conclusion. Likewise, if time runs out and you do not reach a conclusion, you may decide as a group to book additional time to try to complete the exercise, or you have decided that enough lessons have been learned that you want to stop the exercise and review what has already been done and decided.

This leads to the postmortem exercise, which I would recommend be done in a separate meeting, when possible, but we'll cover that in more detail a bit later in this chapter.

Kick Off

Once you have finished preparations for the tabletop exercise itself, it's time to run it! Kicking off a tabletop exercise is generally more structured than just diving into the emergency. As mentioned earlier, you want to build a short introduction that you can present to the participants at the start of the exercise itself. Doing this at the start of the first tabletop meeting will help establish the foundation for the rest of the exercise.

If you are doing this in person, bringing some type of food or beverage to help break the ice can be helpful. This is obviously harder when doing so remotely, but small bribes can go a long way when it comes to overcoming any initial opposition from participants.

One thing that I love to do during the first few moments of getting into a gamified tabletop exercise, especially if the group participating has never done one before, is to give a simple, noncritical situation where you force the use of the dice rolling mechanic before you unleash the disaster scenario upon the group. This could be as simple as selecting one of the participants and say that they felt generous that day, and they decided to bring in some baked goods for the team that morning. This can be followed up by asking them to roll a 1D6. The outcomes for the roll can be as follows:

- 1–3: The bakery ran out of your personal favorite item, so while you had your order filled, you didn't get everything you wanted.

- 4–6: You end up getting an extra treat with your order as the clerk was feeling generous.

The point here is to introduce the gamification element in a benign way. This allows the participants to get a feel for how the mechanic will be used and what happens after a dice roll. As there is no impact to the rest of the exercise, this is a great way to showcase the mechanic in a playful manner. It can also reduce fear and apprehension among participants as they come to realize that the mechanic is straightforward and not overly complicated.

With the introduction of the mechanism out of the way, the next step is to introduce the disaster that is to be overcome. This is up to the conductor to determine how this can happen; it may be that customers are calling in due to an issue with the production environment, employees reaching out due to something they discovered, or a call from an external agency such as law enforcement or the fire department informing you of an incident involving your company.

In any case, the introduction of the disaster should only focus on the initial outcome of that disaster and not the cause of the disaster. The cause will need to be determined by the team at some later point in time, but the goal of the exercise is to first overcome the issue and get back to an agreed-upon state to continue operations. In some circumstances, the root cause can be provided by the conductor at the end of the exercise, so as to avoid unnecessary steps during the exercise itself, unless this is something that has been determined to be "in scope" for the exercise.

Once the situation has been communicated to the participants, you can either select an individual to start the exercise or leave it up to the group to determine who will start. I recommend selecting someone to start the exercise by selecting them as the person who has been informed of the situation initially but reminding the other participants that they are not yet aware of the situation, unless this initial communication was done on a shared platform, such as a group chat or email distribution list. In any case, the question "What would you like to do?" is appropriate to ask at this time.

Running the Tabletop

Once the situation has been provided to at least one participant, then the tabletop exercise itself can begin in earnest. It is up to the participants to continue as they see fit, with the conductor providing guidance in terms of outcomes for decisions made, along with the need to roll dice as appropriate.

One factor to keep in mind is the need to take breaks during the exercise. I recommend taking at least one ten-minute break per hour to help keep the participants engaged. Studies[1] have shown "When students learn or solve problems, attentional resources are depleted; rest breaks may restore cognitive functioning in support of learning." In general, a few minutes for a break is beneficial and less taxing on everyone involved in the tabletop exercise, so ensure these are scheduled and communicated.

If the team is engaged in a deep discussion, feel free to postpone the break until the discussion dies down, but do not skip the break altogether. Be flexible, but don't be reckless either.

Impromptu breaks may be required depending on how the interaction between participants is going. We discussed this in the previous chapter when we discussed strategies in dealing with troublesome participants. Likewise, if a decision has been made that requires a bit more discussion or to determine what an appropriate outcome may be, the conductor may want to call for a break while they research an appropriate outcome or outcomes, depending on the decision. Try to limit these, if possible, to avoid interrupting the flow of the exercise itself, but feel free to use this technique when appropriate.

As mentioned in the previous chapter regarding difficult participants, as the conductor of the tabletop exercise you want to allow your

---

[1] Ginns, P., Muscat, K., & Naylor, R. (2023). Rest breaks aid directed attention and learning. *Educational and Developmental Psychologist, 40*(2), 141–150. https://doi.org/10.1080/20590776.2023.2225700

participants to dictate the pace and decisions that they make. What you do not want to do is have them dictate the outcome of their decisions. This is a common problem that I've seen during exercises, and a gentle reminder that they do not get to determine if their choice was successful or not is usually enough. You can be more aggressive and provide a negative consequence for a particular participant's action if they are a repeat offender, but a reminder should be sufficient.

This leads to another important point; sometimes the outcome from a decision can be negative without requiring a dice roll. This is something you can do to introduce another issue that arises, such as an attacker pivoting to another sensitive system, or a particular control failing, such as a sprinkler system. These secondary issues can come about due to a timed event, i.e., after two hours into the tabletop exercise, introduce disaster X. It can also be due to a decision made by a participant that acts like a trigger. These will still be planned in the mind map or decision tree but may be stand-alone nodes with additional context around them due to their nature of being introduced separately.

Remember, as the conductor you want to keep the team on track, but only provide details for the incident based on what has been discovered thus far. Also remind participants that unless they were involved in a decision, were part of a conference call discussing the situation, or were part of an action done during the exercise, they should act according to the information they have received. Keep the participants on track and let them come to their own resolutions to the problem at hand. You are always able to remind them of the current state of things as well as information they were already made aware of. The only time things become more storyteller-like is when the end of the exercise is reached.

Wrapping Up

Once the exercise has reached the predetermined endpoint, either through a set of decisions made by the participants or due to the maximum time allocated for the exercise, it becomes time to wrap up the exercise.

As the conductor, you should give a short recap of what has been accomplished during the exercise, lessons learned, what worked, and what didn't. This should be brief, as a more in-depth review will be done during the postmortem step, which we will discuss next. Just some highlights would be fine here.

One thing that I personally like to add to these wrap-up moments is providing details on what the root cause of the incident was. In the case of a ransomware outbreak, I will provide details on how the initial compromise happened, how the attackers pivoted through the network, and describe some possible evasion techniques that they may have used.

It is worth noting that going into technical detail like this does require a bit of research depending on the original disaster scenario. The goal is to make it as realistic as possible. This is an opportunity to help tie up the loose ends in the narrative that may be perplexing some of the participants, so providing this level of closure can help them focus on the results rather than wonder how it was all possible.

When providing this root cause information, it may be helpful to speak with some experts outside of the group of participants ahead of time to get an understanding of what may go wrong, thus leading to an emergency or disaster situation. This was covered in an earlier chapter where we discussed how to come up with scenarios to use with a tabletop exercise. Asking people "what keeps you up at night?" is a great way to spark these conversations and can help you determine a root cause that you can build the rest of the exercise from. This wrap-up time allows you to share information with the participants.

If the exercise was not completed in the time allocated, that's fine. Use this time to focus on what remains rather than the root cause disclosure. This is because you may decide to rerun this tabletop again and use the same scenario, using the lessons learned from the first iteration to see if the team can improve. Having pre-knowledge of the cause of the incident will make the exercise less useful as there will be preconceived notions from the participants, which isn't always correct or helpful in a real disaster situation.

Having a short discussion about the exercise at this point is also useful feedback as everything is still fresh in the minds of the participants. Ask what went well, what they enjoyed and disliked, and ask for feedback. This will help make future sessions that much better by understanding what worked with the participants. This can lead to the postmortem exercise, which we will cover in more detail next, but even limiting this discussion to immediate feedback and opinions can be useful before ending the meeting.

Postmortem and Review

After the tabletop exercise is complete, you will want to perform a postmortem to discuss the exercise and write up a report for how the exercise itself went based on your own observations. This document will be the starting point for the next phase, which is the postmortem phase to review the overall exercise and how the participants worked through the situation.

A postmortem review should be scheduled shortly after the tabletop exercise has completed, no more than a few days after the final session. Wait at least until the next day for this meeting to give the participants the opportunity to reflect on the exercise and process what they have gone through. This meeting may be done before or after the report has been written, but in most cases should be done prior to the report being written to incorporate the feedback from the participants.

Make sure to invite the same audience as the tabletop exercise so as to get the most complete review of the exercise itself. Avoid involving other people who were not involved in the exercise so that you can stay focused on the review rather than explaining the exercise from the beginning. The key to this meeting is to be factual and to focus on a few key questions:

1. Was there any missing information that would have been helpful to you?

2. Were any resources missing that would have helped in the situation?

3. Were there any steps missing in the plan?

4. What helped resolve the situation, or if it wasn't resolved, what was the cause for preventing successful recovery from the disaster?

5. What worked well?

6. What needs improvement?

7. Was the disaster recovery plan sufficiently documented?

8. Would a documented plan have helped?

9. How was the communication handled between the teams?

10. Was anything new (techniques, knowledge, etc.) discovered during the exercise that aided in the recovery process?

These are just some ideas on questions that can be asked, but the point is to reflect on the exercise itself, what went well and what didn't. How the team can improve overall, and what changes should be considered. Again, the conductor can lead these discussions but try to keep things factual and focused.

The point of a postmortem meeting is to improve the processes when dealing with a disaster faced by the organization. It is not intended to be a time to point fingers at one another or to call out faults of individuals in their decision-making during the exercise. This is a set of ground rules that should be established at the start of the postmortem meeting.

With the postmortem complete, you can move on to writing the report for those who participated and share it with other key stakeholders who are interested in the learnings and results of the exercise. Use the feedback achieved from the postmortem to assist with this, but also notes regarding the tabletop exercise itself.

Making use of the notes from the scribe is vital here, to ensure no details are missed or misremembered. This report should be as factual as possible; do your best to avoid adding your own personal bias to the report by focusing on the facts that happened during the exercise. This doesn't mean sugarcoating rough areas though. For instance, if there was a confrontational participant that was hostile toward the situation or their peers, then this should be noted and called out in the report. Stating that a decision that you personally wouldn't make or agree with is an example of what should not be included in the report, however.

A modern take on the scribe is to add an AI agent to the session to act as the scribe. While incredibly useful, I would still recommend reviewing any recordings as some subtle actions, discussions, etc., may be "lost in translation" otherwise, but the action of the scribe is the main action you want to be filled.

Provide an overview of what was accomplished, what was discovered and overcome by the team, and what struggles were faced. Describe the consequences of certain decisions but try not to focus on alternatives that should have been taken unless you are explicitly asked to do so. This is more often the case when you act as a consultant to host and execute a tabletop exercise; otherwise, this should be something discussed with the internal group unless you are the subject matter expert in these situations, and even then, these should be suggestions, not mandates. Consider this report the starting point for discussion and a set of recommendations for senior leadership to instigate changes where appropriate. The goal is to better prepare for a disaster, so try to reflect that goal within the report itself.

Depending on the findings in the report, additional meetings may be required to discuss improvements in specific areas. Parts of the report may be required to go into more detail in these areas, so don't be surprised if, as the conductor, you are requested to participate in these discussions.

Tabletop exercises are normally conducted annually and may cover different disasters each time or replay a given scenario until the team "gets it right." Each organization will have their own approach here, but at the very least I would recommend performing at least one tabletop exercise at least annually. For those pursuing SOC 2 compliance, this will be one of the pieces of evidence that the auditors will be looking for, so annual testing may be a requirement.

Tips and Tricks

Over the years, I have learned that no two tabletop exercises are the same, especially when you add gamification to them! But there are some tips and tricks that you can use to help ensure they run smoothly and help you get your feet under yourself to become more confident when running them.

Start Small

If you are new to tabletop exercises in general or are curious about adding gamification to your tabletop skills, it may be overwhelming to start with a large group that spans multiple departments. I would recommend starting with a smaller group, perhaps your own department, and focus on a smaller event that this team would handle on their own. This can simplify the overall planning process and make it much more manageable as you focus on what you already know.

Running a smaller tabletop for two hours with a group of three to five people will be a lot more manageable and approachable than trying a four-hour tabletop with more than ten people from various groups. Follow the same procedures and steps as a larger tabletop but scale it down as appropriate. Also, sticking with a topic you are intimately familiar with can help boost your own confidence in presenting and leading the exercise.

Introduce Gamification Early

As we discussed above, start a gamified tabletop with a noncritical, inconsequential choice from one of the participants to showcase the gamification mechanism. This could be a coffee order, a lunch order, or a random task that they needed to do on their way to work in the morning. It has no impact whatsoever to the rest of the exercise but is a great way to introduce dice rolling and potential consequences, which will lead to early engagement from the other participants.

Always Record the Session

Even when tabletops are held in person, ensure that they are recorded in some manner. Audio-only recording is fine, but having a record of the exercise will be invaluable. Not only does this ensure no details are missed, but you also have evidence in case of a disagreement from any participants at a later date.

While audio recording does negate the need for a dedicated scribe, it is still encouraged that you take notes, which leads to the next tip.

Take Your Own Notes

As a conductor, you should also make notes for yourself during the tabletop exercise. Yes, you can always go back through the recording for specifics, but making note of when an event occurred and at what time it happened will make finding that moment easier when reviewing the recording. Also, noting decisions made by participants will help when you need to clarify work that has already been done or in some cases not been done.

Do not rely on your own memory for keeping track of important decisions and outcomes; keeping good notes can help make the entire exercise a much more pleasant experience for everyone involved.

Expand Your Own Skills

With larger groups, it is inevitable that you will be providing situations that require decisions to teams with skills other than your own. This is true even when planning the tabletop itself, so definitely do not hesitate to reach out to experts in these areas for guidance. I'd recommend against asking those who will be participating in the exercise to avoid spoilers, but some of their peers are great candidates to ask.

The more knowledgeable you are in a domain, the more seriously you will be taken by participants from that domain. This will lead to better participation from other participants if they feel that you understand their domain. It will also help you personally in future tabletop designs, as you will better understand the potential decisions made by members of these domains.

Admit Your Limits

Regardless of how much time you spend in a domain, it's almost inevitable that you will face a situation where you do not know how to handle it. It is better to ask for guidance or assistance from the participants instead and make note of the situation. Yes, I encourage you to broaden your own set of skills, but at the same time being a master of all domains is not realistic, so asking for assistance when you're unsure will often lead to better results than stumbling over potential outcomes instead.

Summary

We covered the basics of preparing for your first gamified tabletop in this one and some tips on running it. We discussed wrapping up the exercise as well as what to look for in a postmortem meeting, along with some pointers on writing the final report. We also discussed some tips and tricks you can use when first starting out in your gamified tabletop journey, which I hope you find useful!

The next chapter is going to be special. We're going to walk you through a tabletop exercise I have done with a group of volunteers. Hopefully, this will be the final push for you to start your own journey, one that helps avoid "the happy path."

CHAPTER 8

Example Gamified Tabletop Exercise

In this chapter, we're going to focus on building out a full gamified tabletop exercise. The full mind map for this exercise will be available at the book's GitHub page (`https://github.com/jsvazic/gamified-tabletops-book`), so feel free to check it out for yourself.

In addition to the sample exercise, I will be including a transcription of a tabletop exercise I did back in 2020 at Tactical Edge. The intention is to provide you with an idea of what a gamified tabletop looks like with actual participants.

The scenario we will be using is a ransomware outbreak, which is by far the most popular scenario I am asked for by clients. This will be a generic scenario, and we will use a somewhat popular-at-the-time ransomware group as the malicious actor. This is intended as an example only and not an actual account of an actual experience encountered by a particular organization.

With all that being said, let's dive into the actual exercise itself. When building out scenarios like this, after building a mind map, I will create a type of "overview document" that I will use as the conductor to provide the narrative, as well as a type of summary of the situation to ensure that I can easily answer questions from the participants. Note that this is optional and not required by any means. I will include an example here, however, to give a more complete picture of what I use when conducting a tabletop exercise with an external client.

© John Svazic 2025
J. Svazic, *Gamified Tabletop Exercises for Effective Disaster Recovery Testing*,
https://doi.org/10.1007/979-8-8688-1252-1_8

Example Tabletop Exercise Summary Document

Company Overview

- The org is a generic software development company, offering a few mobile and desktop applications targeting the enterprise market in some generic market.

- They have a SaaS offering as well, but they still have legacy clients using their on-prem software.

- The company is a Microsoft shop, using Windows laptops, but relying on Microsoft Defender to protect their systems.

- The company being attacked does not have in-house incident response (IR) teams.

- The security team itself is relatively small.

  - No phishing training or endpoint detection and response software (EDRs) in place, and best practices are preached but hardly enforced due to pushback from the rest of the company.

- The company has a cyber insurance policy.

- There are some "concepts of a plan" when it comes to disaster recovery/business continuity, but honestly nothing is centralized, let alone written down.

- The company does have some high-profile clients, which their marketing team uses when they advertise the company's products and offerings.

Pretext

Note   This is background information for the leader of the exercise; it is not to be shared directly with the participants but is meant to provide some background information to help move the exercise along if an unexpected decision is made.

The company has been hit with ransomware. The impact is widespread, and some folks are starting to panic, but details aren't clear as not everyone understands what's happening. Machines are humming as people wait for their login screens to appear, only to receive a strange message. At first report, it seems that most of the office is having trouble/issues, and is reporting it via Slack and email, with employees using their personal devices to communicate their distress.

Intro

Note   This is meant to be a generic introduction but can be targeted to one of the participants of the exercise to get the ball rolling. In this case, a member of the IT or Security team will be selected as the starting participant.

Happy Friday! You wake up refreshed and looking forward to the weekend. It should be a quiet day as you've wrapped up most of your major deliverables earlier in the week, so today should be a catch-up day for the most part, with just some last-minute items to finish off in the morning.

You're still getting ready for the day and decide to prepare some breakfast for yourself. Roll a 1D6 please:

- 1–2: You decide you'll just grab something on the way to work at a drive-through window.

- 3–4: You decide to toast yourself a bagel and make a cup of coffee.

- 5–6: Your significant other has already made a breakfast feast for you! How kind of them!

Before leaving to go to the office, you check your phone and see there's quite a lot of activity in Slack, with people posting about computer issues and a strange "humming" that's happening to the machines in the office before getting a strange message on their computers.

Oh no. You quickly gather your things and head to the office to see what's going on.

When you reach the office, the CEO is already waiting for you asking for an update. *What do you want to do?*

Root Cause

One of the Sales staff received a suspicious email asking them to fill out an NDA for a prospective client. Given that they were having a rough quarter, they jumped at the opportunity thinking that they were lucky to bring back a stalled deal, not paying attention to the sender of the email.

The Word document had macros, which they enabled, as the IT team had re-enabled macros due to their use by other teams in their own internal documents and spreadsheets. This of course resulted in the first stage of a malware payload to be installed, disabling MS Defender and proceeding to infect the machine before spreading to other machines on the network. Most people left their machines at the office as it was easier than unlocking the security cables and bringing them home. Employees returning in the morning reconnected their laptops and went about their morning routine without realizing what was happening until the ransomware note showed up on their computer's screen.

The "Root Cause" section is intended for the end of the exercise, but prior to that the introduction to the exercise is complete, and you can start with the potential decisions that this participant can make. I personally find it easier to start an exercise with a particular participant to see what their first decision would be. Note that in this example, I targeted a participant in the IT or Security team, but sometimes it's better to pick someone who isn't in a technical role, such as Sales or Marketing, to see what their initial decisions would be.

This can be incredibly useful especially when no disaster recovery (DR)/business continuity (BC) plan exists, as you can showcase the importance of having a plan in place and ensuring that employees know who to go to when something goes wrong. In this scenario, it's pretty obvious that something bad has happened, so going to IT/Security first is going to be a natural reaction.

As you can see, we introduce the gamification mechanism, i.e., dice rolling, right away before the main exercise in a lighthearted way. This way, the other participants get an idea of how it works without a complicated introduction or explanation. Also, there is no consequence to a "bad roll," just a less satisfying breakfast.

At this point, you can follow your mind map and continue with the tabletop exercise as we have described throughout the book. Be sure to have fun with these introductions for your participants, and feel free to mix up who gets to kick off the exercise. Again, the purpose of this document is to provide an early script for the conductor and should not be supplied to the participants. Additional information can be added to these notes as deemed necessary, but it is not required.

The "Root Cause" section is essentially a bit of background on what caused the initial situation. This doesn't always need to be provided, as natural disasters do not always have a root cause (i.e., act of God, etc.) or the situation is beyond the company's control, such as poorly maintained infrastructure resulting in flooding, etc.

One thing I will note is to be careful when assigning a root cause to an employee. Best to make them anonymous so as not to build real resentment toward someone over a fictitious exercise. It may sound like this is unnecessary, but sometimes people blur the lines and believe that an individual is capable of being "patient zero" or the main cause of an incident, so a bit of anonymity is worth it to avoid trouble later. But do try to make this realistic, since this will likely be a takeaway to ensure that appropriate defenses are in place in the future, if possible.

As we mentioned earlier, please check out the mind map (in Freeplane format) on the GitHub repository for the book, which you can find here: `https://github.com/jsvazic/gamified-tabletops-book`.

Transcript: Gamified Tabletop Exercise Session at Tactical Edge 2020

The following is a session that I had at Tactical Edge back in 2020. I was joined by the MC and organizer as well as two volunteers to run a sample gamified tabletop exercise. The session was recorded and is available on YouTube. You can find the link to the video here: `https://www.youtube.com/watch?v=i7qxp_mUWcU&t=4s`.

The session was used to demonstrate gamified tabletops, but it also serves as a great example of how one of these sessions are run with live participants. The participants include

Salma: The main presenter and MC of the conference

Ed: The conference organizer

Jen: A security engineer at GitHub and a volunteer for the session

Paul: COO for Blackfire Security, another volunteer for the session

John: Myself, acting as the conductor for the exercise as well as the presenter for the session

Mark: A late joining volunteer and security engineer

I will focus the transcript on the actual exercise and not the introduction to the concept of gamified tabletop exercises or other introductions. I've also edited it slightly to make it easier to follow along. Keep in mind that this was an accelerated exercise, and as such, we will take a lot of shortcuts during the exercise to stay within our session's time limit. Regardless of this fact, this should provide you with an idea on how these exercises may play out. Enjoy!

John: All right, so here's the background on what's going to be happening. The organization that you're working for is a medium-sized company of approximately 450 people. You're a SaaS vendor who is part of a niche market selling services to the waste management industry.

John: You are the industry leader, but there's a lot of fierce competition within the sector itself. There's been a fair share of mudslinging in the market, but you've always managed to stay clean. Now, for the sake of argument, we're also going to assume this is pre-COVID, so you're actually in a physical office together as opposed to being remote. So we're going to take that out of the equation. And that's just for simplicity and the fact that we have 45 minutes left, and we don't have time to work through all the different nuances that could possibly happen.

John: So just so everyone is aware, we're not likely going to finish this scenario, and that's perfectly fine. What we're going to try to do is just showcase what this is actually about. And I want to leave about 10–15 minutes at the end for questions and kind of a wrap-up, which is normally what you do in a regular tabletop anyway. There is no security team, by the way, because there is no perceived need from the senior execs because, again, you're a fairly small company. You've never had an issue before.

John: Why should we pay for a department that doesn't really produce anything? It's just a giant cost center. You know, blah, blah, blah. We have more important things to spend money on. Classic story.

John: So, we have different groups. Who are the groups that we have? We have IT. Paul is going to be representing IT.

John: We have legal. Jen is going to flex her paralegal skills and guide us in that direction. We have marketing. Salma is going to showcase her mad marketing skills. And finally, we have finance. And oh, Ed, great at spending money.

John: Let's see if you can help save some. Let's begin. Good morning. It's a typical Friday, slightly overcast, but normal. Everyone is chugging away at their respective positions without much issue when suddenly the entire building seems to be humming.

John: Hard drives are whirring in an almost eerie unison. Fans are starting to spin up in an effort to keep the systems cool. Approximately ten minutes later, machines start rebooting as if like dominoes. Then all of a sudden after the machines reboot, this happens. Oh no.

John: For those who don't know what this is, this is actually a screenshot from WannaCry, which was ransomware that hit in 2017. Fairly large. This is just an example. You're not actually being hit by WannaCry; you're being hit by another more modern variant. Take your pick.

John: There are hundreds of them that are out there now. But the point is, you've been hit by ransomware. This is what's popping up on all sorts of screens everywhere. Legal. You were in the middle of redlining a few contracts, but you're down now and you can't seem to access them.

John: Thankfully, you printed out a copy for your own records, so you may as well start working on those. Marketing. People are grabbing their phones and checking your corporate website. Obviously, Internet presence is key. We need to make sure that the website is still up.

John: It's slow, but it is loading successfully. So I might as well go ask IT what's going on. Finance. You're in the middle of checking your past due accounts when the outage hit. There seems to be a lot of activity over by the IT help desk.

John: So maybe a coffee break is in order while they sort this stuff out. IT. Your help desk is getting really crowded and the phone is ringing off the hook. People have loads of questions, but you don't have any answers for them yet. What do you want to do?

Paul: All right, so we know we've had this hit some of our computers and servers. Do we know if it's all of them yet or is it just some of them that have had done this?

John: Roll a 1D6 please.

Paul: Six.

John: It seems that it's hit all your desktop machines, and it's hit your email servers as well as a few other systems, but it seems your corporate website has been spared for now.

Paul: Okay. First order of business. We need to figure out where this thing started at because... that makes sense that that machine is going to be the one that's reaching out and hitting the others with the infection. Is there any way for me to identify which machine it started at? I'll say it that way. That's the right way to say it.

John: Roll a 1D6, please.

Paul: Two. No.

John: Awesome. See how easy this is?

Paul: Right, right. I'm keeping my IT hat on, keeping my security hat off. So the next question there is we need to figure out how to stop this from spreading further. If it's only hit our workstations, that's less problematic. What about you said that the website was loading sluggishly right now?

John: Mm-hmm. That's a concern. Possibly more of a concern than the workstations. So while you're trying to figure all of this out, you've got a handful of your employees that are standing around asking, hey, what's going on? What's happening to my machines?

John: You know, marketing has come over, and Selma is very upset. She's like, "Paul, I can't check my email. You know, how do I know what's going on?" And you've got other representatives coming from all over.

John: Jen's wandered over from legal; she's curious. Is there something we should worry about? Obviously, Ed's coming over and saying, why is everyone standing around? What are we paying people for? This is completely inexcusable and balancing things. What do you want to focus on?

Paul: I actually want to focus on finding that source and stopping this spreading further. Because I know that our data center is in danger as well if we can't confirm that it won't spread. And that is where even more value than what we're wasting right now is. So let's see. Do I know if our network is segmented correctly to keep these things from spreading from one network to another?

Paul: Are we all on the same network? Is our server network a different network? What do we do?

114

John: Roll a 1D20, please.

Jen: Me?

Paul: I rolled a five.

John: No, no, just Paul for now. So one thing that I do want to make clear. While Paul seems to be driving a lot of this stuff right now, if any of you others have ideas that you want to chime in on or that you think would be relevant for what you want to do, please let me know, right? And feel free to interject. This is meant to be a parallel exercise.

John: By the way, we just had the late comer join us.

Ed: What is he going to be doing? Oh, OK.

John: Well, Mark, you are going to now take over for finance. And Ed, you're promoted. You're CEO now. Alrighty. So Mark, just roll with it. We've been hit with ransomware. And we're just starting to figure out what to do. So we have Paul, who leads IT.

Jen: Now, John, you did mention that there were other systems hit.

John: Yes.

Jen: Do we know if those have anything to do with employee data?

John: Okay, let's finish off with Paul first. Okay, so you rolled a five, correct?

Paul: Yeah, so I'm definitely—

John: No, you're a nice big flat network.

Mark: I'm so sorry. I was following along live on the other one.

John: That's all right. That's okay, Mark. So this is perfect. So now you know you're in finance. This is normal, right? In the real world, sometimes someone comes in late. I'm going to bring them up to speed really quick. So many stories I can tell about this. Yeah, no, this is perfectly fine.

John: Mark, you're going to represent finance. You've been hit with ransomware.

John: We don't know any of the demands yet, but stay tuned because you may need to get involved. Ed, you've been promoted to CEO. So when people need to make a company-wide decision, they will turn to you.

John: Jen, your question with regard to if any of the systems have PII on them or not. Can you roll a 1D20, please?

Jen: All right. I do not get lucky with these; let me see, 13.

John: 13. So unfortunately, some of the systems that have been infected do actually pertain to some production environments, systems that do have PII for your customers. So you do have potential violations.

Jen: Okay. Do we have customers in California? And do we have customers in the EU?

John: Can you roll a 1D6 twice, please? And let me know what the rolls are for each of them. I can tell you're legal.

Jen: All right. So the first one was a three, and the second one was one. Oh, geez.

John: Okay. So for California, you do not have any clients in California. Unfortunately, you're heavily based in the EU. In fact, that's where the majority of your customers are. In fact, the majority of your customers are in Germany, where it's even better.

Jen: Okay, so we have a 72-hour clock for notifications as far as I know. And again, not a lawyer, paralegal. All right, so that is definitely...

Ed: All right, so I'm going to step in now because I heard we're on a clock now, and I heard in Germany and GDPR; now this little issue is no longer...

Ed: Just IT is corporate, why? So my first question is legal and to finance. Tell me, at what point do we make active our insurance, cyber insurance, to deal with this?

Mark: From a finance perspective, I think we start taking notes for finance right away. We start noticing what we've lost, customers we've lost, downtime we've had, and how we'd like the insurance to replace that.

Jen: And from a legal side of things, I think we have an obligation under our insurance to engage them quickly. We have, I believe, an obligation to use their investigators if we want to be fully covered.

Ed: All right. So I think we should go ahead and start making the phone calls.

John: Ed, can you roll a 1D20, please?

Ed: 1D20. One.

John: So, Ed, I appreciate the fact that you're asking about engaging your cyber insurance vendor here, but you don't have any cyber insurance for this particular type of outbreak. In fact, you barely have cyber insurance that'll cover some sort of data loss. You don't have something that'll cover a ransomware attack because that was something that was on the books, but you decided to push it back.

John: Remember, you didn't have time for this right now, and you didn't see a need for it. So unfortunately, there is no cyber insurance that can help you. You're stuck with what you have. All right.

John: So you're rolling a one.

Mark: Today's the tenth. So I'm hoping our paychecks either went out on the seventh or the first of the month. And I don't have to worry about them until the 22nd or the end of the month.

Ed: That's a bad question because that's finance asking that question.

Mark: You should know. In that case, we don't have to pay again until the first of the month. That's when all our paychecks go out and our bills are due.

John: No, you guys go on a biweekly pay cycle, but it goes out on the 15th and the 1st. So you guys are actually okay for paying your employees.

John: But that is a legitimate question that can come up, right? And that is something that people will want to pay attention to, right? So that's okay.

Paul: Since I've rolled many dice and failed a lot... I'm going to panic at this point and basically go unplug the network stack so that we don't spread infection any further.

John: Can you roll a 1D20, please?

Paul: I'm going to unplug the vacuum cleaner, aren't I? That's what's going to happen.

John: I just want you to roll a die and see what happens.

Paul: Rolled a 10.

John: I'm going to give it to you. We're going to let you go ahead and unplug the system. Unfortunately, 90% of your network has already been infected because this is a fast-moving one. So you did manage to save that last 10%, which was your VoIP system and the coffee maker.

Paul: Good.

John: So you will have coffee, and you will be able to make phone calls, but you can pretty much assume everything else, including the website at this point, is down and encrypted.

Paul: Do we have backups?

John: Roll a 1D20, please.

Paul: 13. Lucky 13.

John: Lucky 13. You do have backups. Yay! Unfortunately, you haven't tested them in six months.

Paul: Well, that's a good time to test them, I think.

John: Isn't it, though? So while Paul is going to go off and test some backups, which, by the way, can you roll a 1D6 and let me know in a minute what that is going to be?

John: Suddenly the news agencies are knocking at your door. Specifically, they're calling Salma's department and saying, oh, hey, so we hear you guys are in the midst of a ransomware outbreak right now. Normally we wouldn't consider this newsworthy, but we got a hot tip that you guys are considering paying the ransom. Do you have any comments about that?

John: What do you wanna do, Salma?

Salma: Maybe these agencies can help us in this critical moment; I don't know.

John: These are newspapers and television studios. Do you really want to accept their help to try to fix an internal issue, or do you want to give some sort of statement for the company?

Salma: Wow.

John: Or better yet, do you want to put Ed in front of the camera, a la a VP or CEO?

Salma: Yeah, I think it's... because it's a big issue, you know? So Ed, please, what do you think?

Ed: Okay. Well, we're on top of the situation. We understand that. This is my canned response. We're on top of the situation. We are engaged with our legal department, and we'll get back to you. That's when it's possible to let you know what's happening.

John: Paul, what did you roll?

Paul: A three.

John: A three. So, your backups don't work. You did find one that worked, but it's about three months old.

Paul: Oh, so we'll lose three months of business?

John: You're going to lose about three months' worth of business.

Paul: Oh, that's fine. How bad can it be?

Ed: Holy crap. Now I'm going to get in there. Wait a second. Wait a second. How come we never, ever, ever tested our backups, Paul?

Paul: That's because I'm writing my resume right now. I've rolled very badly. I've made some bad choices, Ed.

Ed: Oh my goodness.

Jen: No, legal's been up to our eyebrows in contracts. How many contracts and new customers have we onboarded, Mark, in the last three months? That's a quarter's worth of business.

John: Mark, why don't you, before you answer, why don't you roll a 1D6, please?

Mark: Five.

John: So, you only onboarded in the last three months? We're going to give it between the 30 to 50 customer mark.

Mark: That's all. So, 30–50 customers, and that was a good quarter or bad quarter for us?

John: Let's call that a mediocre quarter for you.

Paul: We could ask to re-sign everything, right?

Mark: I mean, that's fine. We certainly could, especially as long as we confirm that we haven't lost any of their private data. It's just our actual systems that are doing the work here that have gone down.

Paul: Yeah, I'm betting that's what that network performance slowdown that the website was having early on probably was.

Mark: That they tried to pull it and couldn't?

Paul: I bet they exfiltrated some data. John, can I roll for that?

John: Yes, you can roll for that.

Paul: A 6 or a 20?

John: Let's do a 20 for this one.

Paul: I rolled an 11.

John: So, you see that the outbound network traffic is definitely higher than normal today, but you do not have visibility into what that data is. You just see from the raw traffic rates tahat it's higher. That's about it.

John: Now, while you're busy taking a look at that, Salma, ringing. Your cell phone rings.

Salma: Yeah. I have my cell phone ringing right now.

John: Yes, your cell phone is ringing. You answer it. And this happens.

John: Hello.

Salma: Hi.

John: This is the group that has ransomwared your systems. We request $150,000 USD sent in via Bitcoin to an email that we will send to you containing our Bitcoin wallet. You have 72 hours to comply before we delete your key. Goodbye.

Salma: Oh, my God.

John: Salma, what do you want to do?

Salma: Oh, my God. This is a fraud. What are we going to do? What are we gonna do? We can't pay all the money and he's I don't think...

John: Well, so far you're the only person who knows how much they're asking; no one else has been told yet, so maybe you want to share with the rest of the group.

Salma: I have to share with Ed.

John: Absolutely.

Salma: Exactly, I just received this call and will reach out to Ed. I'm ringing him.

Ed: I'm not answering. You should roll the dice.

John: No, Ed, you're going to answer a Salma's call.

Ed: Okay. Okay, I'm answering. Hello.

Salma: SOS. We have an emergency. I just received this strange call, like from a group that is the one that is making all this mess and in the system, so they're asking for big money.

Ed: How much?

Salma: A lot of money. A lot of money.

Ed: How much money?

Salma: $150,000.

Ed: $150,000. Wow, wow. So legal. What do you think, we have to do? Let me find out. Legal. If we pay that money, do we have to report?

Jen: Well, we are still investigating as to whether we have obligations to report under GDPR. It's technically not illegal to pay.

Ed: Okay. Well, yeah. If we don't pay, we definitely don't have data for the next three months. For the last three months, we don't have any data. If we pay and it doesn't work…

Ed: All right. So what we know right now, we go with the facts, right? We know 100%. We lost three months' worth of data. Paul, do we know if 100% sure that we have all we lost, that we didn't lose more?

Ed: We lost three months' worth of data, 100% guaranteed? We can recover?

Paul: That appears to be the case, yes.

Ed: Okay. So that's a lot of money. Finance, do we have $150,000 laying around? I think we do because I think that was lower than the premium we were going to pay for cyber insurance, which is why we decided not to go for cyber insurance in the first place.

Ed: So, we played the risk and we're paying for it now. Okay. Okay.

Ed: So, Jennifer, how long will it take us to find out if we pay, if we have to report or not?

Jen: Was the data encrypted?

Paul: Yes.

John: Roll a 1D6, please.

Paul: Me? Or her?

John: We'll get Jen to roll it. She asked the question.

Paul: Oh, okay. Got it.

Jen: Four, John.

John: No, Jen. It was not encrypted.

Paul: I'm having flashbacks over here, guys.

John: Your passwords were encrypted. You guys did a good job by actually using a proper hashing algorithm for your passwords, but the rest of the data itself was not encrypted.

Jen: And as far as the PII, we're talking just email accounts and names?

John: So, for the PII, it would be addresses and names.

Jen: Okay, so we definitely have an obligation under GDPR to report.

Mark: We have an obligation either way, right? Whether we get it back or not, it was lost.

Jen: Yeah, but yeah, since it was unencrypted, we've got 72 hours to...

John: Now I should clarify when I say that it is unencrypted; it means that it was encrypted at rest, but this was an active attack. All right, so this would have been an attack against your network systems where this data would have been in use; thereby, it would have been decrypted at the time of use. So from that perspective, that data itself is unencrypted.

Jen: Unencrypted, yeah.

Ed: All right. So we have lost three months' worth of data. Some of it was unencrypted, and they probably have we don't know a percentage, uh, they're asking $150,000 to unencrypt. We still have to report. We will probably lose a lot of the clients afterward.

Ed: But we'll make it if we pay the ransom we may as a company continue operating correct uh we will limp for a while um.

Salma: Will you trust these guys?

Ed: That was the question I was going to ask as well. Are these people, I mean, do we trust that they will actually be nice people and give us the key or just walk away with the key? It seems like we're a company – we're a company that likes taking risks, right, so we discuss cyber insurance. We say it's too expensive. We'll take the risk.

Ed: And so now we are here on the path that we chose to be in, the risky path. So yeah, the question from Salma is a very good one. Do we trust these people?

Mark: It makes a good argument when we go back to the board next semester or next quarter to argue about how much your cyber insurance costs.

Ed: Yeah, exactly.

Jen: If we can get it after.

Ed: Exactly. How do we go about legally, Jen? How do we go about paying the ransomware?

Jen: We need to investigate how we would do that.

Ed: I think we have the cash available, or do we need to... You keep asking questions. Mark.

Mark: I think we had the cash available in a slush fund. So we said that it was less than the payment. We should have at least that. The hardest part is when the payment doesn't come back, and then we'll find out that we actually took the money out of the employee fund rather than the slush fund.

John: Mark, can you roll a 1D6 for me, please?

Mark: I can. One.

John: So... keep in mind that the industry that you're in is you are making software for the waste management industry, and in North America, the waste management industry is lovingly known to be run by a certain organized group, and you have funds available; uh, those funds however are not necessarily on the books.

Mark: Even better.

John: You may need to gather a loan from your cousin Vinny, for example.

Mark: All my funds are on the books.

Ed: So that's why I forgot about my cousin Vinny. That's why we decided not to purchase the cyber insurance. We have our own insurance.

Paul: But the beauty of this is it can remain totally off the books.

Ed: But again, we still have to... So legally, can we go... And again, this is to Salma as well and Jen. We go and say we were hacked, but the information has been recovered. We contacted everyone within 72 hours, told them, make sure that you change your passwords, blah, blah, blah, blah, blah. But we can say that it was recovered. We don't have to legally say how it was recovered. Is that correct?

Jen: I believe from a legal standpoint, that's... whether we can keep that out of the media.

Ed: The media. Good thing we didn't say anything to the media.

John: Oh, the media is calling again. They're looking for an update.

Salma: Oh, my God. We have to distract the media.

Ed: We're handling the situation with internal processes.

Jen: It's an ongoing investigation that we don't comment on.

Ed: Right.

John: Ed, Ed! People are worried their garbage is piling up at their curbsides, and no one's coming to pick it up.

Paul: I'm going to sneak one of our desktops over to the television station's network and turn it on.

Ed: Oh, okay. That sounds good.

Paul: That'll stop them from bugging us.

Ed: I don't think that's... is that legal, Jen?

Jen: I don't think so. Yeah, probably not advisable.

John: Stay on target, people.

Mark: We were demonstrating for the 7 o'clock news.

Ed: All right. So people are getting worried. Well, we don't have anyone from operations. We need to contact operations and find out what's going on. This didn't affect payroll. Why aren't people doing their work, their job?

John: Well, their desktops are down, Ed. Most of the systems that they're working with daily are not working.

Ed: We can call. Don't we have VoIP services working? Can we get a hold of them and tell them manually or in live, in person, the old technology? Get to work.

John: Let me ask you a different question, Ed. What do you want to do with regard to the ransom?

Ed: Oh, we are going to pay it.

John: So you're going to pay the ransom?

Ed: We have no choice. We'll go with the off the books and pay the ransom that way.

John: Perfect. You pay the ransom. Salma, you managed to coordinate with these guys.

John: I noticed you didn't try to negotiate the ransom down at all, Ed. You know, the ransomware guys really appreciate that. They love getting a nice big windfall that way. And...

Ed: Didn't we say that I know how to manage money?

John: Yes, sure. Absolutely, we did. And after you provide them with the funds and you see that everything has been transferred – silence.

John: And at this point, we're going to wrap up this particular scenario, just because we've got about 15 minutes left.

John: So what really happened? The reality was your company was a target of a corporate espionage attack. Someone, likely a competitor – but as we all know, attribution is hard – hired a group of hackers to steal information from your systems related to your main product. Again, you're providing software for the waste management industry, and part of the reason operations wasn't working, Ed, is because the software that you run is what coordinates the garbage trucks and the waste stations to actually build different departments.

John: This is something, actually, this is drawn from experience that I've had in a previous life where I actually did work for someone who did work in the waste management industry. If that software goes down, the garbage trucks will literally line up for a mile and will start blocking. That's a different story for another day, but, nonetheless, it is a very real-world denial-of-service attack. So the hackers were actually after your IP. They wanted access to the source code.

John: However, the hacking group was also instructed to utilize a scorched earth policy against your organization once they were done. What that means is burn it to the ground. As Jerry Bell, one of our other wonderful presenters, who will be coming later this week, has been known to say, "When your Active Directory gets compromised, just burn it down and start it all over again." That's what these guys were essentially after. They were not there to just ransom your systems.

John: They were there to steal information and then take you down a peg. The goal was, best case, eliminate you from the sector completely. The worst-case scenario as far as this, uh, person or persons who hired this hacking group in terms of their goal was to knock you out of that number one spot so that someone else could take over and become a market leader, so they were out to hurt you and your reputation.

John: Does this sound unrealistic? Because it shouldn't; you know Tony did a great job this morning when he was talking about the DBIR report from Verizon. But again, according to the Verizon DBIR report, 45% of breaches involve hacking, 70% were perpetrated by outsiders, and 86% were financially motivated.

John: You had a hacking attack by a group of outsiders that were paid a large amount of money by a competitor, likely a competitor – again, attribution is hard – who wanted to, uh, become a market leader and take that, uh, financial lead. Here we've got all these things now pointing to corporate espionage. That's normally about a 3% chance of happening as per DBIR for 2020. It's actually dropped over the years – it used to be 17% in 2019 if memory serves – but nonetheless it's not unheard of for competitors to actually harm one another especially in a very tight market. Very commonly distributed denial-of-service attacks and ransomware are often used as distractions to hide evidence of a network infiltration.

John: So, Paul, you did the right thing by saying, hey, I wanted to take a look to see – did we see any exfiltration of the data? There was a bit of an uptick, but part of that could have just been people trying to see what was going on with your systems. The reality is they've been in your system probably for about six weeks, and they've been slowly siphoning data just below that threshold for your alarms to go off because they spent the time to do the research to figure out what was going on. They managed to get in through a spreadsheet with an Excel macro.

John: And that was the initial point of entry. Unfortunately, there wasn't an easy way to track that because it didn't have all the necessary tools that you would normally have if you had a dedicated team.

Ed: So, this is finance's fault.

John: This is not finance's fault. I said it was a spreadsheet.

John: I didn't say it was finance who opened the spreadsheet. It was probably the CEO. One of the security questionnaires from a third party. It could have been a security questionnaire from a third party. It could have been a...

Ed: Hey, would you like to nominate your company for one of the industry awards? Please fill out this questionnaire. I get a lot of those, yeah.

John: Yeah, of course you do. But you guys are the number one market leader.

Ed: Absolutely, it could happen, right? There's many, many different vectors, right?

John: It could have just as well been something from... someone in support who decided to forward an email that they got from their home email address to their work email address and opened it there because they figured they couldn't open it on their home PC. So let's just use one of the work PCs because they're much more powerful and thereby should be easier to do.

John: So that in a nutshell is what a gamified tabletop looks like.

I want to thank you for reaching the end of this book! I've been passionate about tabletop exercises for years, and I'm glad to be sharing my passion with a wider audience. I hope you found this book helpful, and I wish you all the best in your own efforts to improve your own tabletop exercises! May you always have good rolls, and may your disasters be easily overcome. —John

---

Index

A
Average-case scenario, 59, 71

B
Backdoors and Breaches (card
   games), 8
Best-case scenario, 59, 66,
   71, 85
Bitcoin payment, 20
Business operations, 82

C
ChatGPT, 9
Conductor role, 13, 14, 27–29
Conductor's role and their
   temperament, 77, 78
Crafting, 35

D
Data center, 19, 36, 114
DBIR report, 126
Decision Node Editing, 74
Decision nodes, 43, 48, 51,
   70, 74

Decision tree
   description, 40
   example scenario, 41, 42
   flowchart, 40, 44
   options, 43
   process/procedure, 42
   sample, 41
   sample scenario, 43
   tabletop exercise, 43
Denial-of-service attack, 126, 127
Dice, 7, 8, 28, 56
   types, 58, 59
Dice roller, 59
Dice rolling, 90
   mechanics, 66
   outcomes, 66, 67
   recommendations, 65, 66
Disaster scenario, 5, 16, 71, 91, 96
"Discovery" discussions, 83
Dungeons and Dragons (D&D), 58

E
Editing, 52
Emotional distress, 21
Emotions, 19
End goal, 39, 88

J. Svazic, *Gamified Tabletop Exercises for Effective Disaster Recovery Testing*,
https://doi.org/10.1007/979-8-8688-1252-1

Printed in the United States
by Baker & Taylor Publisher Services